FROM VICTIMS TO SUSPECTS

WITHDRAWN
UTSA LIBRARIES

FROM VICTIMS TO SUSPECTS
MUSLIM WOMEN SINCE 9/11

SHAKIRA HUSSEIN

YALE UNIVERSITY PRESS
NEW HAVEN AND LONDON

For information about this and other Yale University Press publications, please contact:
U.S. Office: sales.press@yale.edu   yalebooks.com
Europe Office: sales@yaleup.co.uk   yalebooks.co.uk

Set in Adobe Caslon Pro by IDSUK (DataConnection) Ltd
Printed in Great Britain by TJ International, Padstow, Cornwall

Library of Congress Control Number: 2018959579

ISBN 978-0-300-23042-0

A catalogue record for this book is available from the British Library.

10 9 8 7 6 5 4 3 2 1

For my daughter, Adalya Nash Hussein

CONTENTS

ACKNOWLEDGEMENTS

This book had a very lengthy germination process and so I have a particularly long list of people to thank – many more than I can list here. Those who remain unnamed nonetheless have my eternal gratitude.

First and foremost, I thank all those who agreed to be interviewed during the course of the research for this book. Some are named in the text, but others must remain unnamed.

To Gabriella Sterio who first suggested that I submit a proposal to UNSW Press and to Phillipa McGuinness, Emma Driver and Averil Moffat for editorial support above and beyond the call of duty. Thanks also to Taiba Batool, Rachael Lonsdale and Clarissa Sutherland from Yale University Press.

I undertook the research for this book as a PhD student at the Australian National University and later as a postdoctoral fellow at the University of Melbourne. Thanks to my supervisor Rachel Bloul and to Alastair Greig, David Adams, Andrew Hopkins, Ruth Barraclough as well as Helen Felton and other professional staff at the ANU. At the University of Melbourne, I thank Shahram Akbarzadeh, Lewis Mayo, Nick Thieberger, Lesley Stirling, Charlene Edwards, Abdullah Saeed and Ramila Chanisheff. I also thank Samina Yasmeen from the University of Western Australia, Helen Pringle from the University of New South Wales and Anita Harris from Deakin University.

In Lahore, my thanks to Sadaf Ahmed, Sabir Shah, Rabia Faizy, Mehreen Mukaty, Ayesha Bux, Asif Zaman and his family, and Rubab Hussain and her family.

The theme of this book was developed for the South Australian Women and Gender Studies Annual Public Lecture, which I presented at Barbara Baird's invitation. My thanks to her and to Minerva Nasser-Eddine. I presented a similar lecture in Stockholm, where I was hosted by Zakia Khan and Interfem. My thanks to all concerned.

I covered many of the events explored in this book in articles published by *Crikey*, *New Matilda* and *ABC Religion and Ethics*. Thanks to editors Marni Cordell, Scott Stephens, Cass Knowlton, Sophie Black, and José Borghino. I also explored the topic in journal articles for *Borderlands*, *Australian Feminist Studies* and *The International Journal for Crime, Justice and Social Democracy*. My thanks to Anthony Burke, Mary Spongberg, Scott Poynting and Alison McIntonsh.

The book also benefited from conversations undertaken in the process of co-authoring other work. In this regard, my thanks to Scheherazade Bloul and Scott

Poynting for helpful thoughts regarding Chapter Three and to Camille Nurka in regard to Chapter 5. And to Alia Imtoual for the topic of the book as a whole.

Thanks to Zora Simic, Alia Imtoual, Julie Posetti, Moeen Cheema and Sanaz Fotouhi who read sections of this book and provided feedback. All mistakes are my own.

To old friends from the Canberra Islamic Centre – Kadija Oubelkheir, Jurwina May, Dewi Payne, Azhar Javed, Diana Abdul-Rahman, Kerri Hashmi, Fatima Ahmed, Kate Ahmed, Asmi Wood, Ahmed Youseff and Pak Amin.

To Helen Razer, Kate Gleeson, Rebecca Monson, Samia Khatun and Dakhylina Madkhul. To Nelly Lahoud, Tony Johns and James Piscatori. To Tanja Dreher, Christina Ho, Goldie Osuri, Joumanah El Matrah, Bina D'Costa and Swati Parashar. To Mariam Veiszadeh, Mariam Mukaty, Maryam Rashidi, Ayesha Bux, Anastasia Calendula, Sherene Hassan, Tasneem Chopra, Susan Carland, John Zubrzycki, Sol Salbe, Hana Assafiri, Sudha Seshadri, Aamer Rahman and Nazeem Hussain. To Irfan Yusuf – just because.

To Eugenia Flynn, Alia Kassir, Sarah Malik, Kate Grealy and Maryum Chaudhry, with happy memories of how we desegregated the tent at Café Roza (and to Saeed Saeed for telling us just how world-changing that was).

To sister-act Alia and Fattimah Imtoual.

To Hanifa Deen, Durkhanai Ayubi and all those chasing Sultana's Dream.

To Raimond Gaita, Arnold Zable, and Maria Tumarkin and Randa Abdel-Fattah.

To staff from the RMH neurology, oncology and physio wards, in particular Dr Anneke van der Walt, Josephine

Baker and John Carey. And to Tasneem, whose good humour makes me look forward to my blood tests.

To my family, especially my mother who flew down to Melbourne to help out on the crisis-management front.

But above all, and always, thanks to my daughter Adalya for her patience and fortitude.

PROLOGUE

Dear Adalya,

I've dedicated my book about Muslim women since 9/11 to you not just for the usual reasons that a parent might dedicate a book to their offspring, but because the topic of this particular book has overshadowed almost your entire life. And with politicians and analysts continuing to echo US President Barack Obama's 2015 description of conflict with the so-called Islamic State as a 'generational struggle', it's a topic that seems destined to dominate all our lives for a long time to come.

You were only five years old on 11 September 2001. Even though our apartment in Canberra was about as far from New York and Washington as it is possible to get, when I saw the news on the television late that night, I went through to your bedroom to make sure that you were still safely asleep. Amid all the uncertainty about the future, it was immediately clear that Muslims around the world would feel the consequences of al-Qaeda's crimes.

A couple of weeks later, I left you with your grandmother in Australia while I travelled to Pakistan to try to work out how any of us were going to manage life in the strange new post-9/11 world. Friends in Pakistan were horrified that I had left you in Australia. They had heard reports about Muslim women in the West having their headscarves torn from their heads, and about the firebombing of a mosque in Brisbane. It isn't safe for Muslims to live in the West anymore, they told me. Bring your daughter back here – we'll find you a job in a posh girls' school. A Pakistani journalist suggested that we could move to Abbottabad, the town where he had grown up. It was a popular holiday destination, a beautiful location with good schools. And it was a military town, so it was very safe.

But Pakistan has been a frontline state in the War on Terror, and Abbottabad eventually turned out to be the hiding place of Osama bin Laden. Although we've spent time with other Muslim women and girls in locations ranging from Lahore to London and Paris to New York, we've spent the post-9/11 years as Muslims living in Australia.

Back when you were in primary school, we enjoyed many happy trips to the South Coast with a group of friends from our local Islamic centre. We were a diverse little tribe whose family backgrounds ranged from Lebanon to Morocco, Indonesia to Australia. Some of the women wore hijab and some did not, but we all enjoyed a trip to the beach. And we were all shocked by the footage of the riots at Sydney's Cronulla Beach in the summer of 2005, when Muslim women and girls were attacked and abused alongside their menfolk.

After Cronulla, Muslims stepped up their efforts at reconciliation and bridge-building, with women playing a key role. Muslim women pitched in with the catering at interfaith dialogue events, gave interviews to media outlets, organised fashion shows in an attempt to answer people's questions about Muslim women's dress codes. Many of us campaigned on multiple fronts – against the mandatory detention of asylum seekers who arrived by boat, against the introduction of ever more stringent anti-terrorism laws, against the apparently endless wars in Afghanistan and Iraq.

And after each new terrorist attack, each new crime committed by one of our coreligionists, we explained. We explained that most Muslims were horrified by such events, we explained that Islam is a religion of peace, we explained how Muslim women (particularly those whose faith is made visible by their headscarves) were coping with the impact of discrimination and harassment. We explained and explained and explained. We explained to politicians and policymakers and journalists and total strangers on public transport who noticed a signifier of our religious identity and asked us to explain the role of Islam in every-thing from international politics to the application to build a new mosque in the neighbouring suburb.

Women in all communities are conscripted into the role of peacemakers and healers. It's a role that many willingly undertake, but, after nearly a decade and a half, even the most tireless Muslim women are growing weary of explaining crimes which we did not commit and events over which we have no control. And such explanations have become an expectation. If we don't explain, we are asked to explain why we've failed to do so.

I was away from home for work when the news broke that Donald Trump had won the 2016 US presidential election. Just as on 11 September 2001, I felt the need to make sure that you were safe and sound, that you had not somehow come to harm as a result of an event on the other side of the world. This time, I had to settle for text messages instead of tiptoeing into your bedroom to check on you.

And then I opened my laptop and got back to the never-ending task of explaining what the news meant for Muslim women.

You have grown up listening to this low hum of explanations and you've also done more than your fair share of explaining. I hope that my book may help to lighten this burden of explanation – if only by explaining why we ought not to be expected to explain.

Love always,
Mum

INTRODUCTION

In February 2001, an 18,000-strong crowd gathered at Madison Square Garden for a gala benefit performance of Eve Ensler's *The Vagina Monologues*. Audience members had paid up to $1,000 per ticket to see stars such as Jane Fonda, Brooke Shields and Gloria Steinem read Ensler's work, recite pet names for their vaginas, and join Glenn Close in a chant of 'Cunt! Cunt!' On stage, talk-show host Oprah Winfrey recited 'Under the Burqa', a new mono-logue that Ensler had written especially for the occasion. Then the stadium went dark to throw the spotlight on Zoya, a young member of the Revolutionary Association of the Women of Afghanistan (RAWA), clad in the burqa she had brought to New York at Ensler's request. Zoya later described how the blinding spotlight brought tears to her eyes as she slowly made her way onstage, where '[s]lowly, very slowly, Oprah lifted the burqa off me and let it fall to the stage'.

Zoya's speech about Taliban oppression of women in Afghanistan received a standing ovation from the audience.

The burqa-clad woman in the photo circulated by Australian senator Jacqui Lambie in September 2014 does not look like a shameful statue waiting to be unveiled. Like the woman in Ensler's monologue, she is swathed in a huge piece of cloth, but she stands straight and tall, a string of prayer beads hanging from her wrist as she points a pistol towards an unseen target. And she is not about to receive a standing ovation. Rather, the image, which originated from the Facebook page of the right-wing anti-immigration party Britain First, was emblazoned with the message 'Terror attack level – Severe: an attack is highly likely. For security reasons, it's now time to ban the burqa.'

Embarrassingly for Lambie, the woman in the photograph turned out to be not a dangerous terrorist, but a heroine of law and order. Afghan policewoman Malalai Kakar had worn the burqa to conceal her identity in the course of her work combating violence against women, until she herself was murdered by the Taliban in 2008. Photographer Lana Slezic described Lambie's use of her work as 'insensitive and frankly stupid' and noted that '[Kakar] was the pinnacle of strength in Kandahar at a time that was extremely difficult for Afghan women. She was the first female police officer in Kandahar and stood for the rights of women.' Lambie unconvincingly claimed to have known this all along. 'Malalai Kakar would have been the first to agree with my call to ban the burka. Far from desecrating her memory, my Facebook post honours her and the deadly struggle against brutal thugs and extremists.'

How has the woman beneath the burqa been transformed from a helpless victim unable to cast off her own shroud into a menacing terrorist who must be brought under control 'for security reasons'?

Orientalist discussions on gender and Islam have long fluctuated between portrayals of Muslim women as hapless victims in need of rescue and as dangerous agents of an alien ideology in need of discipline – a pattern that has become more pronounced during the post-9/11 era. As the Taliban retreated from Kabul in 2001, the sought-after media money-shot was that of 'liberated' Afghan women casting off their hated burqas. By the time Jacqui Lambie posted the image of Malalai Kakar, the narrative had shifted from the forcible imposition of burqas in Afghanistan to the introduction of state-imposed burqa-prohibition in European states including France, Belgium and the Netherlands. This modification in attitudes towards the burqa reflects a shift in representations of Muslim women from that of passive victims in their own societies and communities to active participants in Islamism and the 'Islamisation' of the West. Unruly Muslim women must, it seems, be controlled in order not only to liberate them from their own false consciousness, but also to contain the threat they pose to Western societies.

The role of Muslim women is endlessly malleable to suit the political needs of the moment. Donald Trump's promise to withdraw US troops from Afghanistan and then his later decision to maintain them were both reportedly framed in terms of women's dress. In October 2015, Trump told a rally in New Hampshire: 'We want it where the women over there don't have to wear the you-know-what [hand-sweep across face]. And then I said, well that makes sense. That's nice. And then I saw them interviewed. They said "We want to wear it. Why would anyone tell us not to? We've worn them for a thousand years." They want to! What the hell are we getting involved for?'

After all, he went on to note, wearing a burqa would save women the time and hassle of putting on make-up. Online magazine *Salon* headlined its report of this speech with 'Donald Trump defends the burqa – in the most sexist way possible.'

After coming to office, however, Trump came under pressure from the foreign policy and military establishment to abandon this isolationist outlook and stay the course in Afghanistan. And according to a report in the *Washington Post*, one of the factors that convinced him to send further troops to a war that he had long complained was 'wasting our money' was a photograph presented to him by his then national security adviser H. R. McMaster. The black and white snapshot taken in 1972 showed three smiling young Afghan women walking down a street in Kabul dressed in miniskirts and high heels. This, McMaster told him, illustrated that 'Western norms had existed there before and could return'. For Trump, the sight of the miniskirts apparently outweighed the influence of the Afghan women whom he had earlier ventriloquised as describing the burqa as their choice.

The function of Muslim women, then, is to serve as useful props in whatever presentation has been scripted by the lead performers. And, of course, their costumes are far more important than their voices.

Imperial Feminism

In November 2001, nine months after Zoya's ritualised unveiling in Madison Square Garden, United States First Lady Laura Bush made a now-famous radio address to the nation in a slot usually occupied by her husband. Her purpose, she announced was:

> to kick off a worldwide effort to focus on the brutality against women and children by the Al Qaeda terrorist network and the regime it supports in Afghanistan, the Taliban.
>
> That regime is now in retreat across much of the country, and the people of Afghanistan, especially women, are rejoicing. Afghan women know through hard experience what the rest of the world is discovering: The brutal oppression of women is a central goal of the terrorists.

Laura Bush's speech in support of Afghan women was part of the effort to broaden the focus of US retaliation to include the Taliban as well as al-Qaeda. But it also served as a mission statement for the plethora of subsequent operations to rescue Muslim women not only in Afghanistan, but also throughout the Muslim world and in Muslim communities in the West. The so-called War on Terror, in all its many incarnations, was to be a war with gender at its heart.

The deployment of 'imperial feminism' in response to patriarchal conflicts long pre-dates 2001. Gayatri

Spivak, an academic at Columbia University, coined the famous phrase 'white men saving brown women from brown men' to describe the British colonial endeavour to rescue Hindu women from death by *sati* (self-immolation on their husband's funeral pyre) – and white women such as Laura Bush have long played an important role in bolstering such civilising missions. In her book *The Eloquence of Silence: Algerian Women in Question*, Marnia Lazreg describes an infamous 1958 episode in which French officers in Algiers held a public demonstration to show local support for French rule. Held just four years before Algeria gained independence, the demonstration included a ceremony in which local women were solemnly unveiled by French women. Lazreg observes that 'to unveil women at a well-choreographed ceremony added to the event a symbolic dimension that dramatised the one constant feature of the Algerian occupation by France: its obsession with women'. Similarly, Joan Wallach Scott points out the parallel between Bush's radio address and the 'racist benevolence' of those French feminists who sought to rescue their unfortunate 'immigrant sisters' rather than address patriarchal power structures in their own society.

The fear of terrorism, which was so acute in the wake of the 9/11 attacks, has been revived by subsequent attacks in locations as wide-ranging as Bali, Madrid, London and Boston and more recently by the departure of hundreds of young Muslims from Europe, North America and Australia to join the self-declared Islamic State in Syria and Iraq. And terrorism is no longer an exclusively male domain, with women participating in attacks or planned attacks in locations including San Bernardino, Mombasa, London and Jakarta.

However, the threat supposedly posed by Muslim women is not limited to the 'security reasons' referred to in Jacqui Lambie's call to ban the burqa. Alongside the fear of Islamic terrorism is a growing fear of Islam as a cultural hazard that is gradually undermining Western societies from within – and Muslim women, the transmitters of Muslim cultural practices, are held to play a key role in this infiltration. Furthermore, their 'chosen' subservience supposedly threatens to reverse the gains made by generations of feminists in the West, reopening questions that had been considered resolved.

But what to Western eyes appears to be 'subservience' is not always the case: the vision of patriarchy as a system inflicted on women by men may be a simplistic view. Author and academic Deniz Kandiyoti, whose research explores gender relations, describes the 'patriarchal bargaining' practised by Muslim women. By negotiating a path within the parameters of an apparently patriarchal structure individual women are able to shape their role in a way that suits them, and many Muslim women have played the role of disciplinarian as well as disciplinee.

Muslim Women as Explainers

Lila Abu-Lughod, a professor of anthropology at Columbia University whose work focuses on the issues of power and women's rights in the Middle East, has described how in the weeks following the first lady's speech she was deluged with enquires from journalists asking her to use her knowledge of gender and Islam to 'explain' the unfolding conflict:

> Instead of political and historical questions, experts were being asked to give religious or cultural ones. Instead of questions that might lead to the examination of internal political struggles among groups in Afghanistan, or of global interconnections between Afghanistan and other nation-states, we were offered ones that worked to artificially divide the world into separate spheres – re-creating an imaginative geography of West versus East, us versus Muslims – cultures in which first ladies give speeches versus others in which women shuffle around silently in burqas.

Experienced academics such as Lila Abu-Lughod were not the only ones to find themselves inundated with requests – which often took the form of thinly veiled demands – to 'explain' the post-9/11 landscape in terms of Islam's treatment (or mistreatment) of women. Muslims living in the West found themselves conscripted to provide such explanations on a daily basis. Muslim women, however, found themselves in a paradoxical situation in which they were simultaneously silenced and called upon to speak out. On the one hand, Western politicians, journalists and feminists as well as male Muslim community leaders took it on themselves to speak on Muslim women's behalf, as though they were incapable of speaking for themselves. On the other hand, Muslim women's voices were in very high demand – but only insofar as their message could be shaped to serve the purposes of their audience.

The widespread initial response of many Muslims (including Muslim women) to the 9/11 attacks and the outbreak of the War on Terror was to 'explain' their faith and to distance themselves from the extremists who had committed mass murder in its name. And Muslim women went on to explain that they were not oppressed by their religion, using themselves (their education, their confidence, their healthy relationships with friends and family) as evidence. They acknowledged the oppression suffered by Muslim women at the hands of patriarchal regimes in the Muslim world but stressed that such practices were grounded in culture rather than religion and that those best positioned to address such issues were Muslim women themselves.

It is broadly acknowledged that the headscarf makes women targets for harassment and abuse but less noted is its magnetic attraction for those seeking explanations about anything regarding Islam. Most obviously, of course, they're asked to explain the headscarf itself. But they're also the go-to source for explanations on everything ranging from the war in Syria to the detention of Muslim asylum-seekers by Western immigration departments to Muslim religious practices such as fasting during Ramadan plus the Muslim perspective on the moral panic du jour. And Muslim women who don't wear the hijab are not exempt from this gruelling emotional labour, once their religious identity is discerned via other signifiers or in conversation – only they have to begin by explaining why they don't wear the scarf.

In Australia and elsewhere in the West, public discussions on Islam and gender have focused on Muslim women as victims (whether of Islamic misogyny or racist harassment and violence) and Muslim men as perpetrators (whether of rape, terrorism or domestic violence). With Muslim men perceived as embodying a dysfunctional masculinity, women have assumed a vital role as bearers of identity and defenders of communities.

In their 2007 book about Muslim-American youth identity, Selcuk R. Sirin and Michelle Fine note that:

> Young men and women seemed to operate in two quite different social psychological fields. The young Muslim men walked in the shadow of the label of *terrorists* and heard comments like 'They hate women'; 'They hate Christians'; and 'They are really violent'. Young Muslim women, in contrast, walked in the shadow of the label *oppressed*.

These different social psychological fields produced quite different responses from the young people concerned, with young Muslim men hesitant to speak to express their opinions in terms that might attract an even higher level of suspicion while young Muslim women described having acquired a forthright mode of expression in response to the perception that they are silent, passive victims of their religion and community.

This obligation not merely to 'speak' for their communities but to 'embody' a positive image of Islam is an expression of women's role as defenders of their communities. The positioning of 'successful' (generally defined as educated, professional, fluent in English) Muslim women as 'positive embodiments' of Australian (or European, or American) Islam is meant to reflect not only on the women themselves, but also on the families and communities to which they belong. Just as the 'backwardness' of Islam is said to be embodied by oppressed, downtrodden Muslim women, the 'positive' face of Islam is embodied by successful, articulate Muslim women. Such women are presented on public platforms as the antithesis of the oppressed Muslim women of popular stereotype. And, of course, if Muslim women are not oppressed then Muslim men are not oppressors.

Highlighting the achievements of successful Muslim women is a useful tactic in counteracting perceptions of Muslim women as passive victims, unable to speak for themselves. However, more problematically, it also tends to take as self-evident the belief that 'successful' women must be the products of healthy and supportive social networks. Such women, it is implied, are too well educated, too independent, too strong, to be 'victims' of gender oppression. While it is undoubtedly true that many Muslim women benefit from belonging to supportive networks, this line of defence reinforces misplaced stereotypes of victimhood. Gender discrimination and violence are not confined to any particular social class, nor to the ranks of the lowly educated. Nor is 'victimhood' necessarily made visible by a meek, submissive social manner.

The rise of the so-called Islamic State (also known as ISIS, ISIL and Daesh) has seen an even greater demand for Muslim women's voices as both Muslim and non-Muslim governments adopt the strategy of 'countering violent extremism' – which almost always refers only to Muslim extremism despite the rise of violent white nationalism in Europe, North America and Australia. And, in the struggle to counter violent extremism, Muslim women are no longer regarded as passive and helpless. Instead, they're seen as crucial figures who can offer important counter-narratives in the struggle against Islamic State.

The heightened visibility of the far right, as illustrated by developments such as the return to parliament of Pauline Hanson's One Nation party in Australia, the election of President Donald Trump in the United States and Brexit and the strong showing by far-right parties in elections across Europe, has added impetus to what Sara R. Farris terms 'femonationalism'. In her 2017 book *In the Name of Women's Rights: The Rise of Femonationalism*, Farris describes a convergence of 'three very different political actors – right-wing nationalists, certain feminists and women's equality agencies, and neoliberals [who] invoke women's right to stigmatise Muslim men in order to advance their own political agenda'. Farris focuses on western Europe, but similar trends are visible in North America and Australia.

In the fraught post-9/11 atmosphere, Muslim women who spoke out about gender abuse within their communities had their voices either appropriated or selectively quoted. Faced with these hazards, many women chose to remain silent or to speak out only within what they regarded as safe, internal spaces. For many Muslim women living in Australia, the issue of when to speak and when to keep silent reached crisis point with the sermon delivered by the then mufti of Australia, Sheikh Taj al din al Hilali, during Ramadan in 2006. As reported by *The Australian*, Hilali's Arabic-language sermon notoriously compared scantily dressed women to 'uncovered meat' left out where it might tempt any passing cats. 'Whose fault is it, the cat's or the uncovered meat? The uncovered meat is the problem.' Coming in the wake of the so-called 'Sydney gang-rape trials', Hilali's sermon sparked an international furore as well as tensions among Muslim women living in Australia about how best to respond. While there was near-universal condemnation of the sermon itself, many female members of Sydney's Lebanese Muslim community believed that his subsequent apology ought to be the end of the affair and urged us to take our concerns to the Sheikh himself rather than air them publicly. Others (myself included) felt unable to confine our criticisms to the designated internal spaces, despite the fear of handing ammunition to those who were hostile to Muslims in general.

Egyptian-born journalist Mona Eltahawy denounced this silencing effect in her book *Headscarves and Hymens*. Eltahawy rose to international prominence for her coverage of the so-called Arab Spring and its aftermath, during which she was beaten and sexually assaulted by the security forces in Cairo. According to Eltahawy, Arab and

Muslim women's rights activists like her find themselves caught between 'a bigoted and racist Western right wing that is all too eager to hear critiques of the region and Islam that it can use against us' and 'those Western liberals who rightly condemn imperialism and yet are blind to the cultural imperialism they are performing when they silence critiques of misogyny'. She hotly denies the accusation that 'I want "the West" to rescue "us"' but does not fully address the fact that Muslim women are subjected to rescue whether or not they ever asked for it. Trapped in the double bind between racism and misogyny, women who condemn misogyny committed by Muslim men (or 'hang the dirty laundry', as Eltahawy describes it) find their voices appropriated by one side or the other – or both – despite their often strenuous objections.

Nor does silence provide an escape from this double bind, as illustrated by the experience of Gold Star mother Ghazala Khan, whose son US Army Captain Humayun Khan was killed by a suicide bomber in Iraq in 2004. Khan stood silently at her husband's side at the Democratic convention in 2016, while he made a speech noting that, under then presidential candidate Donald Trump's proposed ban on Muslim immigration, their son would not have been admitted to the country for which he later sacrificed his life. Addressing himself to Trump (who is widely known to have evaded military service), he declaimed, 'You have sacrificed nothing and no-one.' In an interview with ABC News, Trump retorted, 'If you look at his wife, she was standing there. She had nothing to say. She probably . . . maybe she wasn't allowed to have anything to say. You tell me.'

Ghazala Khan later responded that her husband had asked her whether she wanted to speak but that the sight of her dead son's photograph projected onto the wall of the convention centre had left her in too much pain to do so. 'When I was standing there, all of America felt my pain without my saying a single word. I don't know how he missed that.'

How then are Muslim women to respond when so much is read not only into every word that they speak, but also into every word that is left unspoken?

Samuel Huntington's influential 1992 essay 'The Clash of Civilizations' frightened and angered me with its forecast of bloodshed along the civilisational fault line between Islam and the West. In the wake of the 9/11 attacks, Huntington's us-versus-them language seemed to be making his grim worldview into a self-fulfilling prophecy. And, as Laura Bush's speech illustrated, gender norms play a crucial role in the conflict-driven civilisational definitions.

Fired by a quixotic compulsion to hold back the clash of civilisations, then, I took advantage of the sudden interest in the issue of Muslim women by persuading an Australian newspaper to finance my travel to Pakistan on the basis of my links with local Afghan and Pakistani women's organisations. Like Abu-Lughod, I had ambivalent feelings about assuming this role. On the one hand, it arose from an oversimplified and stereotyped misreading of Muslim norms. On the other hand, I welcomed the opportunity to address those stereotypes – and I was also desperate to travel to Pakistan, to bear witness to the fallout from the conflict, to reconnect with the women I knew there and to grapple with what we were learning to call 'the post-9/11 world'. The first two chapters of this book are based on the research that I undertook in Pakistan with the Revolutionary Association of the Women of Afghanistan (RAWA) and with the women's wing of the Pakistani Islamist political party, the Jamaat-e-Islami. The remainder of the book focuses on the experiences and perspectives of Muslim women living in the West, although it continues to reference events in Muslim-majority societies.

In the early stages of my research, I regarded feminist campaigns in Muslim-majority societies and anti-racist campaigns undertaken in the West as two entirely separate spheres in which different tactics, language and discourse could be deployed. I set aside my concerns about the simplistic and often racist reports and campaigns on behalf of Afghan and Pakistani women, so long as they adequately communicated the magnitude of the crisis these women were facing.

However, the events of 2001 illustrated the perils of that outlook. In Australia, the attacks in New York and Washington had been immediately preceded by the so-called 'Tampa Affair', in which the Australian government refused permission for the Norwegian frigate MV *Tampa* to enter Australian waters with the 433 refugees (most of whom were fleeing Taliban persecution in Afghanistan) that it had rescued from their sinking vessel. On the issue of asylum-seekers, sympathy for Afghan women was far outweighed by fear of their husbands, brothers and fathers – fear which had been stoked by sensational and reductive media coverage and support campaigns. And, as discussed in chapter one of this book, after the September 11 attacks, the 'Stop Gender Apartheid in Afghanistan' campaign was readily appropriated for the purposes of the War on Terror in a synthesis of feminism and militarism.

While Muslim women living in the West and their co-religionists in Muslim-majority societies face very different challenges, then, their fates remain closely inter-woven. Muslim women campaigning against anti-Muslim racism in the West are frequently accused of indifference to the plight of their co-religionists living under patriar-chal regimes in Muslim-majority societies such as Pakistan and Afghanistan. Conversely, regulations targeting Muslim women's religious dress in France and elsewhere in Europe are cited by religious conservatives in Muslim-majority societies as evidence of Western hypocrisy and double standards in the area of women's rights. And, of course, many women live transnational lives that traverse the civi-lisational boundaries between Islam and the West.

The figure of the Muslim woman has long provided Orientalism with one of its favourite metaphors – that of veiling and unveiling – in which the Orient is the seductive, veiled object of the Western project to unveil and reveal. However, the dynamics described in this book are not specific to Muslim women. Muslim women have become the arche-type of the 'Third World Woman' as described in Chandra Talpade Mohanty's landmark essay 'Under Western Eyes: Feminist Scholarship and Colonial Discourse'. Similarly, Sara R. Farris has observed that, while feminists and women's organisations have directed their femonationalism at Muslims in particular rather than at migrants in general, for right-wing nationalist parties Muslims are a subset of a broader campaign against immigrants and immigration. Finally, while it is important to focus on the specific issues facing Muslim women rather than collapse them into a false universal category of womanhood, contemporary narratives about Muslim women also reflect underlying gendered assumptions about the nature of female identity and the role of women during conflict. Women are expected to remain passive and docile, yet support the wars and campaigns fought on their behalf. To consort with the enemy, let alone to fight alongside them, is a betrayal of both your tribe and your gender.

1

AFGHAN GIRLS

Civilised people throughout the world are speaking out in horror – not only because our hearts bleed for the women and children in Afghanistan but also because in Afghanistan we see the world that the terrorists would like to impose on the rest of us.

– Laura Bush

Steve McCurry's 'Afghan Girl' was perhaps one of the most memorable images of the Cold War, as well as *National Geographic's* most successful cover photograph. Her face framed by a tatty red scarf, the Afghan girl with the striking green eyes gazes straight into the camera. Published in 1985 with the caption 'Haunted eyes tell of a refugee's fears', the photograph of the unnamed girl in a refugee camp in Pakistan allowed viewers to inscribe the image with their own chosen narrative of Afghan suffering under Soviet occupation. Nearly two decades later, the magazine described this photograph as 'a searingly beautiful image of a young girl with haunting eyes who came to symbolise the plight and the pain and the strength of her people'.

The Afghan Girl vanished from view in the years after her photograph was published. Her name and her fate remained unknown for nearly two decades. Perhaps that was appropriate. After the Soviet withdrawal from Afghanistan in 1992, the nation whose fate she represented also vanished from the international radar, overshadowed by a confusing mess of civil war, tribalism, landmines, leftover Cold War weapons and grudges.

Zala was not an orphaned child like the Afghan Girl, but she was still touchingly, heartbreakingly, young. Nineteen years old and still in high school, she spoke of democracy, liberation, women's rights, duty. When we met in Peshawar in August 2000, she had already proved her dedication by secretly returning to Afghanistan from Pakistan in order to gather evidence of the Taliban's human rights abuses. She said that she wasn't afraid to die for her cause.

Zala was a member of the Revolutionary Association of the Women of Afghanistan. RAWA was formed in 1977 and had campaigned against Soviet occupation, CIA-backed factions and the various warlords who battled for control of Afghanistan after the fall of the Soviet-backed regime in 1992. But it was RAWA's struggle against the Taliban that gained them international recognition.

Like so many others, I had discovered RAWA via its website. For many years, RAWA had used its magazine

Payam-e-Zan to communicate with Afghans; after the Taliban took power in Kabul, their website gave them a global audience at a time when, at last, information about Afghan women was highly sought after. RAWA shared testimonies from women and girls who were denied access to healthcare and education under Taliban rule, and covertly recorded evidence of Taliban punishments. One widely circulated video showed the public execution of a burqa-clad woman in the Kabul soccer stadium. 'If you are freedom-loving and anti-fundamentalist, you are with RAWA,' the banner of their website proclaimed. This proclamation was a powerful appeal to the desire of many women in the West to show solidarity with Afghan women.

I had expected that my first meeting with Zala would consist of a discussion over a cup of tea. Instead, she led me out to an ambulance that would transport us back to the refugee camp on the outskirts of Peshawar where we shared a room for the next several days. The camp was a mudbrick-walled fortress surrounded by a moonscape of brick kilns set up to exploit the pool of cheap labour. The brick kilns brought employment, but also a fine, choking dust that polluted the water supply and caused chronic respiratory problems among the children and the elderly. The camp's residents – men, women and children alike – told stories of homelessness, bereavement and trauma inflicted by various forces during decades of war and displacement.

My encounter with Zala took place during a critical time for Afghanistan but also at what would come to be regarded as a key moment for international feminism. As reports of Taliban abuses against Afghan women emerged, Western feminist organisations, including the US-based Feminist Majority (FM), had launched a political campaign to isolate the regime and publicise its excesses. This engagement by Western feminists with the oppression of 'Third World' women was unprecedented in scope and scale. In its early phases, the campaign presented a challenge to US foreign policy before being appropriated wholesale in the wake of the 9/11 attacks, when the mission to rescue Afghan women became a *raison d'être* for military intervention in Afghanistan.

Soviet Storm to Taliban Tyranny

By 1996, when the Taliban seized control of Kabul, Afghanistan had suffered nearly two decades of Soviet occupation – which had been fiercely resisted by loosely allied groups of guerrilla fighters, the *mujahideen* – followed by four years of brutal civil war. The United States had chosen to work through the Pakistani secret intelligence agency, the Inter-Services Intelligence (ISI), to supply military aid to the *mujahideen*. The ISI, in turn, favoured the Pakistani Islamist party, the Jamaat-e-Islami, and its Afghan ally, the Hezb-e-Islami, led by Gulbuddin Hekmatyar. More moderate forces within the Afghan resistance were marginalised, with the tacit agreement, if not outright approval, of the United States.

In a 1998 interview with *Le Nouvel Observateur*, Zbigniew Brzezinski, one of the main architects of this strategy, and US National Security Advisor to President

Jimmy Carter, justified its consequences by asking the rhetorical question 'What was more important in the world view of history? The Taliban or the fall of the Soviet Empire? A few stirred-up Muslims or the liberation of central Europe and the end of the Cold War?' Sociocultural anthropologists Charles Hirschkind and Saba Mahmood report the words of one CIA analyst: 'Fanatics fight better.' These 'stirred-up Muslims' and 'fanatics' subjected Afghan women working for international aid organisations to constant intimidation, seriously disrupting the provision of welfare and education to Afghan men, women and children living in refugee camps in Pakistan. However, in the proxy war between the United States and the Soviet Union, the *mujahideen* were cast by Western media, and in government propaganda, not as violent patriarchs but as colourful heroes in the struggle against communism.

In launching the Feminist Majority's 'Stop Gender Apartheid in Afghanistan' campaign in 1997, its chair Mavis Leno (wife of talk-show host Jay Leno) claimed: 'Until September of 1996, Afghan women, particularly those living in cities, were highly involved in public life. They wore contemporary clothing, participated in the government and worked in all professions, particularly as doctors, nurses, lawyers and teachers.' This remarkable historical amnesia erased discussion of the culpability of US foreign policy in arming and empowering misogynist warlords during the years of counter-insurgency, rendering the Taliban as a purely 'Afghan' problem.

The years of civil war following the Soviet withdrawal and the fall of the pro-Soviet Najibullah government in

1992 further eroded women's welfare. The weapons that flowed so freely into the region during the years of Soviet occupation were now turned against the Afghan population. The West's erstwhile proxy, Gulbuddin Hekmatyar, shelled Kabul into ruins. It is little wonder that when the Taliban began its advance, promising among other things to end the sexual abuse of women and boys by the warlords they displaced, many Afghans – women as well as men – initially made it welcome.

The Taliban advance initially received rather muted international press coverage, and even some positive reports of the new militia's desire to cleanse the country of warlord corruption and brutality. However, after the fall of Kabul in 1996, reports soon emerged of the regime's attempts to impose an extremely repressive code of behaviour upon women, enforced by the Department for the Promotion of Virtue and the Prevention of Vice. These edicts ranged from the deadly – forbidding women to seek medical help from male doctors, while curtailing the ability of female doctors to work – to the merely petty (if grim), such as the edict enjoining women to walk noiselessly upon the streets least male passions be aroused by the sound of their footsteps. Women were denied the right to work and study, and to go out in public unless accompanied by a male relative and dressed in the burqa that covered their entire body except for a mesh screen at eye level. Those found disobeying even trivial injunctions risked humiliation and injury from beatings in the street. The US-backed *mujahideen* had issued similar ordinances during the years of counter-insurgency against the Soviet Union. However, in the post-

Cold War era, Afghan militias were no longer regarded in the West as allies and freedom fighters whose less savoury foibles could usefully be ignored. Unlike previous misogyny against Afghan women, Taliban abuses succeeded in generating a transnational feminist response.

The Feminists Rally

The feminist campaign against the Taliban was multifaceted rather than unified or centralised and significant shortcomings have since been identified. Most of them arose out of one prominent strand of the broader movement – US-based Feminist Majority's 'Stop Gender Apartheid in Afghanistan' campaign. This campaign was able to position itself as a fashionable celebrity cause, emerging as the most high-profile international public response to Taliban misogyny. Philanthropist Mavis Leno was enlisted as chair and political figures such as Hillary Clinton and Madeleine Albright added their voices to the growing condemnation of the Taliban.

If the symbol of Afghan suffering under the Soviet occupation had been the unflinching gaze of the green-eyed girl, the symbol of Taliban oppression was the face hidden behind the blue burqa. Campaigners, journalists and celebrities lined up to gain an insight into the lives of Afghan women by trying on the tent-like garment themselves and Feminist Majority sold small pieces of burqa mesh to wear as a 'Symbol of Remembrance for Afghan Women'. But in interviews Afghan women (including RAWA members) tended to accord much less symbolic weight to the burqa. They were more preoccupied with other, not necessarily gender-specific, issues – the loss of close relatives, homes and farms; the struggle to subsist when the means of subsistence had been destroyed. When they did talk about the burqa they used quite different language to that deployed by their self-appointed Western saviours. While some urban-educated Afghan women complained of the burqa in aesthetic or ideological language, most women talked about more practical considerations. Low-income women complained about the economic burden of purchasing an extra garment, or the fact that if a household could not afford a burqa for each of the women in the house, they could not all go out at the same time. Some women objected not because they opposed covering up per se, but because the burqa was not their preferred style of veiling. Such women may have resented having the burqa foisted upon them, but had no desire to unveil entirely. For others, the enforcement of the burqa either reflected existing social practice in their location or was worn for security reasons that were not confined to the Taliban.

The transnational feminist movement intervened at an important political moment. In the aftermath of its conquest of Kabul, it appeared likely that the Taliban could eventually become recognised as the legitimate government of Afghanistan. The country's fragmentation during the years of occupation and war had long impeded trade and development initiatives throughout Central Asia, but a new, stable government might enable fresh political and business deal-making. With the Taliban's rise to power allowing the reopening of important and long-closed trucking routes, it was hoped that by 'normalising' the Taliban as a government like any other, stalled business ventures could proceed. Clinton administration officials indicated that they would be prepared to recognise a Taliban government if they negotiated a truce with the Northern Alliance and agreed to 'modify their behaviour' on women's rights.

However, as the regime failed to consolidate its control of the country and its abuses against women became a prominent feminist cause and media story, this outcome became increasingly unlikely. This was illustrated by the failure of the UNOCOL pipeline – a proposed trans-Afghanistan pipeline to convey gas from Central Asian countries through Pakistan to the Indian Ocean – which would have provided the Taliban with revenue of between US$50 million and US$100 million a year had it proceeded. As UNOCOL executives courted Taliban officials, feminist lobbyists successfully pressured the Clinton administration to withhold its endorsement – a campaign that was reported in a 1998 *Washington Post* article by foreign correspondents Dan Morgan and David Ottaway. The project was repeatedly put on hold and finally shelved after the United States targeted Osama bin Laden in missile strikes on Afghanistan in August 1998. And, after the strikes on New York and Washington in September 2001, opposition to the Taliban, as called for by the Feminist Majority campaign, became official US foreign policy.

The Women of RAWA

At first glance, RAWA's activists and their US admirers seem to share little common ground. The RAWA women have not forgotten that the United States supported their bitter enemies for many years – for instance, Gulbuddin Hekmatyar, the warlord responsible for the bombardment of Kabul and, initially, the Taliban itself. But RAWA's website, the courage of its members in documenting Taliban atrocities, its newly formed links with Western feminist organisations and media appearances by English-language proficient young women – who were, even with their faces veiled for security reasons, extremely photogenic – all helped to make it the most prominent Afghan women's organisation in the West, despite its relatively marginal position among Afghans themselves. RAWA's success in seizing the political moment during the years of Taliban rule was in part due to its members' single-minded determination in gathering compelling evidence of Taliban abuses and their adroit communication skills. However, it also reflected RAWA's willingness to reframe its political identity when dealing with outsiders and to perform to certain required stereotypes, even as it sought to overturn them.

RAWA was founded by Meena Keshwar Kamal, generally known simply as 'Meena', in 1977. The organisation's origins and independence remain controversial, in part because of Meena's marriage to Faiz Ahmad, leader of the Maoist Gruh-e-Enquilabi (Revolutionary Group or RG), later known as the Sazman-i-Rihayi. RAWA supporters maintain that the two organisations were and are entirely separate. However, the description of RAWA as Maoist in origin comes from some admirers such as author Hafizullah Emadi as well as many of its enemies. RAWA members themselves generally dismiss any Maoist tag as irrelevant.

But, while RG has fallen into obscurity, RAWA has gained in prominence and standing, in large part because its branding as a feminist organisation gained it a far broader international support base.

After the Soviet invasion in 1979, Kamal and most other RAWA members joined the millions of Afghans who sought refuge in Pakistan and Iran. They established schools, literacy classes and orphanages, and continued to circulate their publication *Payam-e-Zan* (Message of Women). All of these projects placed a heavy emphasis on women's empowerment. Politically, RAWA set itself firmly against the Soviet occupation and its puppet government in Kabul, but also against the *mujahideen* who were the favoured beneficiaries of United States and Pakistani military aid, and who were exerting ever-greater control over the running of the refugee camps in which more than 2 million Afghans now resided.

In 1986, Meena Kamal's husband Faiz Ahmad was murdered in Quetta, reportedly by agents of Gulbuddin Hekmatyar. A year later Kamal, too, was murdered by agents of the Afghan secret service. She remains a revered figure within RAWA; her portrait hangs in their schools and offices and her poetry is recited at their functions. The RAWA website describes her as a martyr and her murder is cited as justification for the continued security conscious-ness maintained by the organisation today, including their reluctance to publicise the addresses of their projects and the concealment of their leaders' identities – measures which rival organisations regard as an affectation or as evidence of a sinister hidden agenda.

The post-Soviet era consolidated the power of RAWA's powerful warlord enemies, especially Hekmatyar. But the suffering of Afghans during the civil wars of the 1990s received little international attention. For the most part, feminists outside the region were similarly oblivious to the abuses against women committed by the various forces fighting for control of the country.

The rise of the Taliban simplified the Afghan story for Western audiences. And, as the new regime attracted international condemnation for their particularly attention-grabbing brand of misogyny, the undercover feminists of RAWA began to receive more attention.

Although the initial momentum was slow, RAWA's cyber-campaign eventually began to generate media and feminist interest. After discovering RAWA's website, Eve Ensler, author of *The Vagina Monologues*, travelled with RAWA to Peshawar in northern Pakistan and across the border to Afghanistan and wrote a series of articles on her experiences for the glossy magazine *Marie Claire* and other publications. Feminist Majority invited RAWA to attend its 'Feminist Expo 2000' in Baltimore and assisted touring RAWA members in gaining media exposure. An appearance by RAWA on the Oprah Winfrey show led to so many hits that the RAWA website collapsed. A logo on the homepage read 'Welcome, Oprah viewers.'

Having gathered the raw data needed to make their case, RAWA was very skilful in dealing with the media and international campaigners. They made journalists' work easier by directing them towards good stories and supplying them with documentation and footage. They had polished, English-speaking representatives available for interviews. But, more than this, many Western activists and journalists described their encounters with RAWA in terms suggestive of seduction. Eve Ensler's description of herself as 'completely smitten' illustrates a very common reaction. The willingness of often very young, fragile-looking women to put themselves in the front line was part of this emotional appeal. But RAWA was also very skilled at giving outsiders a sense of being part of their struggle, using their security procedures to make international supporters feel chosen and trusted.

My own initial contact with them followed what appears to have been the established pattern – initial contact by email, in which RAWA advised that I should let them know where I was staying in Peshawar so that they could contact me there, followed by the very short initial meeting with Zala and then transport by ambulance to the camp where RAWA's projects were based. I cannot see how RAWA could have made any definitive assessment of me from this screening, beyond that of gut instinct. Nor did I ever hear of any interested journalist or researcher being denied contact with RAWA during the pre-9/11 period in which international exposure and support was both vital and difficult to come by.

However, this screening process and the sense that one had to be judged worthy before being entrusted with access to RAWA members imparted a sense of privileged access that the writers concerned did not hesitate to highlight to their audience back home. Anne Brodsky, a psychology professor and frequent visitor to Afghanistan writes:

Because RAWA is an underground organization facing grave security risks, this book would have been impossible without years of established trust between the organization and me.

...An outside researcher could not have been allowed to live with RAWA, permitted inside the organization, nor meet the number and range of people that I did.

Similarly, Eve Ensler described how 'we [Ensler and her photographer] met them in a hotel in Pakistan where they interviewed us to decide if they would take us into their clandestine world. Then they made the decision to trust us and took us in.'

Ensler's enthusiasm for RAWA and her fame as a writer left a deep impression on the young RAWA members I met in Pakistan not long after her visit. They said that Ensler had asked to join the organisation, but had been told that only Afghan women were eligible. (Separate international support organisations were later established.) In asking to join RAWA, Ensler seems to have been unaware both of the requirement for Afghan nationality and the nature of the commitment that RAWA demands of its members. Women cannot simply join RAWA by applying: they must go through a lengthy application process to convince senior RAWA members of their commitment and their value to the organisation. This was brought home to me after I asked Zala whether the women attending a RAWA literacy class were RAWA members. 'These are just illiterate village women. How can they serve RAWA?' She added that

32

women 'like that' were also unable to join RAWA because they would not be able to gain the support of their families. A woman's RAWA activism requires a very high level of family support, since members may have to relocate according to the needs of the organisation.

Even though (as Ensler discovered) non-Afghans could not join RAWA, they were nevertheless made to feel like insiders. This sense of acceptance can be hard to come by in transcultural feminist movements, where disputes over 'ownership' of a struggle are common. Comparing my encounters with RAWA with meetings with various other Pakistani, Afghan and Indonesian feminist activist groups, one of RAWA's most distinctive traits was their gift for intimacy. Zala and I shared a bedroom during the week that I spent at the camp, and other RAWA members joined us there to talk late into the night about their formative life experiences, their political beliefs and their hopes for the future. They were unashamed to share the degree to which the personal was political and to invoke connections between themselves and their non-Afghan listeners. When I asked one young RAWA activist whether she was afraid during her clandestine trips to Taliban-era Afghanistan, she replied: 'It is my duty. And it is your duty to help us.'

Taking their cue from Zala and other RAWA activists, the women and girls living in the camp shared testimony of loss and grief, as well as their hopes for a better future. They talked nostalgically about life in Afghanistan where their families had had homes and farms 'with a garden full of grapes' – although for many of them this was a second-hand nostalgia based on stories told to them of a time before they had been born. While the international campaign against the Taliban focused on its crimes against women and girls, the women themselves spoke about the injuries and injustices committed against their male family members and their grief for dead or missing fathers, husbands and sons. One young woman told me that her greatest source of unhappiness was the gruelling hardship that her brothers were forced to endure as labourers in the nearby brick kiln while their mother and sisters lived relatively sheltered lives at home.

The Taliban were not the central protagonists in many of these stories of loss. In some cases, the culprits were members of the Northern Alliance. Other women had suffered at the hands of abusive family members or from destitution and exploitation. This became obvious during a wedding which Zala and I were invited to attend during my stay at the camp.

Even though the bride's face was coated in a heavy layer of make-up, it was possible to see that her expression was frozen in a rictus of fear. Her eyes were blank and seemed not to take in any of the scene before her – the wedding guests, the foreign visitor, the women who sang and laughed in a vain attempt to draw her into the celebration. It occurred to me that she might have been given a drug of some kind to calm her down.

The mother of the bride was nowhere to be seen. And when the other women explained why, they dropped all pretence of celebration:

The girl's mother is in another room, crying. The family is newly arrived from Afghanistan and they have nothing. They can't afford to feed everyone, so they had to find a husband for their daughter. She is only 16, and she is marrying an old man. He already has a wife his own age, and just a few months ago he married another young woman. It is not what anyone wants for their daughter, but what can they do? They cannot take care of her themselves and they cannot find a husband of her own age.

I could see why that terrified young bride's family might have felt that they had no alternative other than to hand her over to an old man so that she would be provided for and her share of the family resources could be shared among their other needy offspring. Islam's early years were also characterised by war and displacement, and the religion's endorsement of polygamy is intended as a means to provide women with male protectors and providers during times of high insecurity when their usual providers may have been lost to conflict. But I could also understand why the mother of the bride could not bring herself to join the celebrations.

The public execution in Kabul's soccer stadium of a woman known only as 'Zarmeena', filmed by a RAWA member from under the cover of her burqa, was eventually to become a symbol of Taliban atrocities. The footage is shaky and often obscured by the fabric under which the camera is hidden, but it is haunting nonetheless. Three burqa-clad women – two of them apparently guards, the third woman their prisoner – are delivered to the stadium in the back of a red pick-up truck. Turban-clad men with guns circle as the guards lead the prisoner across the soccer field and kneel her down at the edge of the penalty box. A female police officer who had guarded Zarmeena in the years before her death later told journalist Anton Antonowicz that the condemned woman had believed until almost the last moment that she was to be subjected to a flogging but that as the mother of seven children, she would be spared death. A young child can be heard crying in the hum of conversation from the crowd in the stadium as Zarmeena turns to plead with the man who is holding a gun to her head. Reportedly, her own children were among those who watched from the stadium as the shots rang out, her body pitched forward onto the ground, and the other two women returned to straighten her burqa over her corpse.

The image eventually became detached from the event itself, so that many of those who viewed it assumed that Zarmeena was being executed for a crime of 'immorality', such as adultery. In fact, Zarmeena had been convicted of murdering her husband. This was a crime that in some circumstances could have rendered her liable for the death penalty in the United States too, although her marriage's allegedly abusive history as reported by Antonowicz and others might have proved a mitigating factor. The footage did not gain immediate media traction, but as stories about Afghan women became more newsworthy the execution of Zarmeena became a major story not only for the brutal manner of her death, but also for the 'backstory' of how it was secretly recorded from beneath the burqa – a symbol of oppression turned into an instrument of resistance. This backstory, however, often went unreported, as many networks screened the footage without attributing it either to RAWA specifically or to Afghan women activists more generally.

RAWA was more than willing to take advantage of the Western fetishisation of the veil in order to further its campaign. Zala was anxious that I should get all the photos necessary for my story and correctly assumed that, for a Western audience, this would include pictures of women in veils. None of the women in the camp used burqas in their everyday life (though most used chadors), so a search was made and a couple of crumpled burqas were found (their condition in stark contrast to the women's other clothes, which were generally immaculately cared for, even if often old and worn). A couple of women were prevailed upon to don them, their self-consciousness rendered invisible by the enveloping fabric, and a baby and a few toddlers were rounded up to make the image complete.

Despite my deep discomfort at some of the overtly orientalist imagery involved, my belief at the time was that it might be desirable, even necessary, to deploy misplaced stereotypes about Islam and Muslims in the face of such a serious level of oppression. Concerns about Islamophobia, which loomed large in the lives of Australian Muslims, including myself, seemed very remote during my conversations with Afghan women in Pakistan. Here, the immediate enemy were violent patriarchal militias. Many Afghans felt that the outside world, which had taken such an interest in them when they had been the brave guerrillas fighting Soviet imperialism, had afterwards abandoned them to their fate. They were not overly concerned if Western media reports and support campaigns (which of course most Afghans never saw for themselves) were ahistorical, Orientalist or racist, providing that they adequately communicated the prevailing sense of crisis to the outside world.

But, of course, the campaigns against the Taliban and racism in Australia did not operate in separate spheres at all – in fact, they related to some of the same individuals. Reductionist portrayals of Afghan gender relationships heightened Western fear and suspicion of Afghan men, fear which had very concrete repercussions when Afghan refugees attempted to find sanctuary in the West. In Australia, the arrival of 'mainly Muslim' asylum-seekers, many of them Afghan, was greeted with political and media hysteria. Two notorious incidents – the 'Tampa' incident in which a Norwegian cargo ship, which had rescued a sinking asylum-seeker vessel, was refused permission to land in Australia, and the 'children overboard' affair in which the Australian government falsely accused asylum-seekers of throwing their children into the ocean in order to force the Australian navy to rescue them – had a decisive effect on the outcome of the 2001 election. Voters re-elected a conservative government under the slogan, 'We will decide who comes to this country and the circumstances in which they come.' Mental illness, self-harm and suicide attempts were rife among asylum-seekers held for years in desert prisons – problems that became even more acute after the 2012 reintroduction of offshore detention on Manus Island, Papua New Guinea and

Nauru. On the issue of immigration and asylum, sympathy for Afghan women was (and remains) far outweighed by fear of their husbands, sons and brothers.

Aftermath of 9/11

In the weeks following 9/11, the 'Stop Gender Apartheid in Afghanistan' campaign dovetailed with the propaganda campaign supporting the US-led Operation Enduring Freedom in a synthesis of feminism and militarism. As Feminist Majority said, 'By mid-November, the Bush administration was giving speeches that could have been directly lifted from the organisation's literature.'

Many feminists, Afghan and non-Afghan alike, were disturbed to have their cause appropriated by US militarism. RAWA in particular expressed vehement opposition to both the Northern Alliance and to the US-led intervention. Three days after the September 11 attacks, RAWA posted a statement on its website headlined: 'The people of Afghanistan have nothing to do with Osama and his accomplices.' After expressing their condolences to those who had lost loved ones in New York and Washington, and noting that 'bin Laden has been the blue-eyed boy of the CIA', the statement continued:

Now that the Taliban and Osama are the prime suspects by the US officials after the criminal attacks, will the US subject Afghanistan to a military attack similar to the one in 1998 and kill thousands of innocent Afghans for the crimes committed by the Taliban and Osama? Does the US think that through such attacks, with thousands of deprived, poor and innocent people of Afghanistan as its victims, it will be able to wipe out the root-cause of terrorism, or will it spread terrorism even to a larger scale?

The effects of the US-led military intervention in Afghanistan were already visible when I arrived in Peshawar in October. Newly arrived refugees, reluctant to seek help from established agencies for fear of being returned to Afghanistan, roamed the streets in search of shelter and sustenance. I found my way to the hospital where some of those injured in the bombing had been brought for treatment. On the desk of the doctor in charge of their care lay a pile of folders, each marked with the single word 'WAR'. Dr Rahim told me that there had been eighteen patients, and two deaths.

Fifty-five-year-old Daud Muhammad, from Jalalabad, was crushed when a missile landed less than ten metres from his home. He died a few days after being admitted to the hospital. Thirty-year-old Reza Muhammad, a farmer, was passing Jalalabad airport on his way home when he was hit by shrapnel. He, too, died soon after reaching Peshawar. A member of the medical staff recalled: 'He had a head injury, but also he had severe psychological trauma. He kept saying over and over "There was a bang, there was a flash, and then my friends were dead . . ."' The other war casualties included women and children, and a member of the UN demining mission, which lost four staff in the bombing of Kabul.

Maryam Marao's family were shepherds, living in a village outside Jalalabad. Their daughter had been married three months earlier and had gone to live in another village, Karam, two hours away on foot. Then came the night Karam was bombed. As Maryam recalled: 'At 3 a.m. we heard a blast. We thought it was an earthquake. We could see it from our village. Everyone rushed to Karam. Five in my daughter's house were killed. Two children, two young women and one old man.' Her daughter survived but with multiple injuries, and was evacuated to Peshawar.

When the Taliban escorted a select group of foreign journalists across the border to Karam to witness the impact of the bombing, they were met by angry villagers waving shovels and sticks. But Maryam, thin and drawn, wrapped in a black headscarf, seemed more bewildered as she described that night:

> The Americans should know they acted wrongly. They have killed a lot of very poor people. In every home in Karam, there are at least one or two dead. All the rest of the village has moved to the plain near our home. They are living there in bad conditions, in makeshift shelters. Their own homes, their livestock, are all gone.

A year earlier, RAWA activists had needed to work tirelessly to generate media attention for their cause; now they were swamped with more enquiries than they could hope to address. They had become the go-to contact for any story about Afghan women, regardless of whether or not it was relevant to their organisation. When one of their members came to meet me at my guesthouse in Islamabad, she was mobbed by other journalists who were eager to speak to her and arrange further interviews with RAWA. When we eventually reached my room, her mobile phone rang with a call from a journalist eager to make contact with the woman who had reportedly run a secret beauty salon in Kabul, which, as my interviewee explained, was not a story that RAWA knew anything about. For her, it was more important to explain why RAWA believed that, rather than liberating Afghan women and girls, the US-led military intervention would only leave them at the mercy of a different set of oppressors.

A few weeks later, the Taliban were driven out of Kabul. Western media and audiences expected Afghan women to celebrate their newfound freedom by casting off the supposedly hated burqa, ignoring the fact that many women wore it for reasons of their own. And Sharbat Gula, known previously only as the Afghan Girl, 'a young girl with an unforgettable fire in her eyes', turned out to be one of them. With Afghanistan back at the centre of global politics, photographer Steve McCurry and a team from *National Geographic* set out to rediscover 'the face that ha[d] haunted him for years' (and had propelled him to international fame). Seventeen years after the original photograph was taken, the documentary film *Search for the Afghan Girl* revealed how McCurry and the *National Geographic* team used a network of contacts as well as 'cutting edge eye-scanning and facial-recognition technology' to track down and identify the middle-aged woman whose childhood photograph had featured on so many postcards, calendars and fundraising brochures. Married in her early teens and the mother of four children, she told the interviewer that she had never felt safe. 'But life under the Taliban was better. At least there was peace and order.' Although uncomfortable talking with an unrelated male like McCurry, she allowed herself to be photographed with her burqa drawn back to reveal her face and her famous green eyes. But, she told McCurry, 'It is a beautiful thing to wear, not a curse.'

The tension between RAWA and Feminist Majority became public in 2002 when FM purchased *Ms* magazine and introduced themselves to its readers with a supplement that focused on the organisation's role in the struggle for Afghan women's rights. The supplement's smug tone, its failure to mention RAWA, and its relegation of other Afghan women and organisations to supporting roles prompted a US RAWA supporter to post a scathing open letter on RAWA's listserve, from where it was widely circulated. 'Could it be that they are ignorant of a time period before Afghan women were somehow newsworthy? Are they unwilling to report on this period of time in which they, like the rest of the world, were complicit in ignoring the pleas of our Afghan sisters for aid?'

The Afghan women had, of necessity, been treading a fine line. Critiques that champion RAWA at the expense of Feminist Majority tend to describe RAWA as active agents of resistance in relation to the Taliban and other misogynist forces within Afghanistan, but passive victims when it comes to the appropriation of their cause by Feminist Majority and United States foreign policy. However, despite its strong anti-imperialist ethos, RAWA was an active (if not equal) partner with Feminist Majority and other Western-based media and women's organisations – a partnership that depended to a large extent on eliding the question of its own ideological standpoint. RAWA's efforts to conform to a worldview palatable to Western liberal feminists and media consumers rendered it vulnerable to appropriation. This was not a role that the organisation was prepared to tolerate on a long-term basis. Once the Taliban had been overthrown, RAWA's outspoken criticism of the newly installed Afghan government and the ongoing pres- ence of International Security Assistance Force (ISAF) troops saw it sidelined in favour of more compliant partners.

'What happens if we leave Afghanistan?'

The bombing of Karam village seemed like a momentous event when Maryam Marao described it to me in Dr Rahim's office in 2001. However, it was quickly overtaken by stories of other bombings, other civilian casualties, and eventually another war, this time in Iraq. Yet again, a global superpower had become trapped in an apparently endless war in Afghanistan with no victory in sight. In 2010, the whistleblower website WikiLeaks released a huge cache of secret US military reports which highlighted both the carnage of the war in Afghanistan and the continued public relations value placed upon the testimony of Afghan women. The files revealed that, during 2004–9, hundreds of Afghan civilians had been killed in unreported incidents involving troops from the NATO-led ISAF, while over 2,000 more had died in the Taliban's roadside bombing campaign. And a memo titled 'Afghanistan: Sustaining West-European Support for the NATO-led Mission: Why Counting on Apathy Might Not Be Enough' warned that 'fragile' levels of European public support for the military campaign 'might turn into active hostility' if military and civilian casualties continued to increase. Noting the 'pervasive skepticism among women in Western Europe towards the ISAF mission', the memo noted that 'Afghan women could serve as ideal messengers in humanizing the ISAF role in combating the Taliban' and suggested targeting Afghan women's testimonials towards shows that attract 'large and disproportionately female audiences'.

Less than a month after the publication of WikiLeaks' Afghan war logs had reignited debate about the half-forgotten conflict, the face of another young Afghan woman came to symbolise the need for the United States and its allies to stay the course in order to protect her countrywomen from a resurgent Taliban. The 2010 cover story in *Time* magazine headlined 'What Happens If We Leave Afghanistan' was illustrated by a photograph of the face of a young, unveiled woman 'liberated' from her burqa but gruesomely disfigured, her nose and ears sliced away. Eighteen-year-old Aesha Mohammadzai had been jailed for the crime of running away from her abusive husband and in-laws and then subjected to the even worse punishment of mutilation upon her release. Her punishment was inflicted by her husband and his family, reportedly under the authorisation of a local Taliban commander. Her father took her to a US military base near their home, which delivered her to a women's shelter in Kabul where she was introduced to *Time* photographer Jodi Bieber.

Introducing the magazine's 'powerful, shocking and disturbing' cover photograph, *Time* editor Richard Stengel told his readers that the disturbing image was meant to contribute to the debate about the war that had been ratcheted up by the release of the WikiLeaks Afghan War Diary:

> We do not run this story or show this image either in support of the U.S. war effort or in opposition to it. We do it to illuminate what is actually happening on the ground.

Asked whether she agreed with the comparison of her work to McCurry's 'Afghan Girl', Bieber answered: 'Oh definitely. For me, it was a matter of putting a moment of history in perspective. It was just one thing that added to the image. I think there are quite a few layers to it.' And the most prominent layer in *Time*'s cover story was that the withdrawal of US troops from Afghanistan risked abandoning women to similar acts of horrific abuse by the Taliban.

However, as Moon Charania points out, the implicit claim that the withdrawal of IFAS troops would leave more Afghan women and girls to suffer a similar fate to Aesha omits the fact that her mutilation (and the events leading up to it – her marriage at the age of fourteen in order to settle a family feud, the years of violence and servitude at the hands of her husband and in-laws, her arrest and imprisonment when she tried to leave their household) had all taken place in a region of the country that was supposedly under the control of the Afghan government rather than the Taliban. Despite its well-established record of violence against women, the Taliban itself denied responsibility for what they described as the 'barbaric' attack upon Aesha and in an article for *The Nation*, journalist Ann Jones wrote that the Taliban did not feature at all in the account that Aesha provided to her a few weeks before the publication of the *Time* magazine cover. Regardless, the photograph of her injured face supplanted the burqa as a symbol of Taliban oppression.

The non-government organisation (NGO) Women for Afghan Women, which had introduced *Time* magazine to Aesha, arranged for her to be taken to the United States to undergo reconstructive surgery on her damaged face. But a 2012 follow-up story by CNN reporter and writer Jessica Ravitz on 'Saving Aesha' provides glimpses of a young woman infantilised and institutionalised by her well-intentioned American rescuers. Aesha received a celebrity welcome to the United States and was fitted with a temporary prosthetic nose. But she soon began to exhibit erratic and challenging behaviour that led to her eventual hospitalisation – not for the promised surgery, but for psychiatric treatment. She was diagnosed with both post-traumatic stress disorder and borderline personality disorder, and her doctors ruled that she was still too emotionally fragile to undergo such a major procedure.

After her discharge from hospital, Women for Afghan Women provided Aesha with round-the-clock care from a team of social workers and roommates at their head-quarters in New York. However, her difficult behaviour continued. Knowing that her story and her mutilated face were valuable fundraising assets, she resented her limited access to spending money and suspected her self-appointed guardians of cheating her. Her roommates burned out at a high rate until eventually she announced that she was leaving the NGO's care to live with an Afghan family in Maryland whom she had met via one of their members. Her spurned rescuers feared the worst. But, once settled in an environment of her choosing, Aesha's moods settled to the point where she was able to come off her psychiatric medication and prepare to undergo the surgery for which she had come to the United States in the first place. As it turned out, Aesha did not need a team of social workers and doctors as much as she needed a family.

In an interview on CNN, Ravitz and the host Jonathan Mann expressed their admiration for Aesha's strength as a survivor of torture, but also their wonderment at her 'child-like' behaviour:

'It's heartbreaking – and to see that image of her swinging on the swing like a child – she's 22 years old. What kind of shape is she in emotionally?'

'She is very childlike. She's someone who sees an ice-cream truck and runs after it.'

'At age 22.'

'Yes, she's very childlike. She'd never gone to school a day in her life. She came to the United States knowing so little – she did not even know that there were days of the week.'

As an object of rescue, then, this traumatised but basically resilient woman is depicted as an innocent and ignorant child. Yet exercise equipment in parks is basically playground equipment for adults, and students Aesha's age running after ice-cream trucks would not be regarded as an unusual spectacle on university campuses. Aesha's story illustrates the continued linkage of rescue missions to US foreign policy, as well as the ways in which such missions can go astray when women are not permitted to dictate the terms of their own salvation.

More than three decades after her first appearance on the cover of *National Geographic*, Sharbat Gula was once again enlisted to reflect the shifting fortunes of the millions of Afghan refugees dislocated by war. However, in October 2016 the famous green eyes stared out not from a glossy magazine, but from a mugshot released by Pakistani officials when they announced that the Afghan Girl had been arrested for holding false identity documents.

As Human Rights Watch reported, in the second half of 2016 Pakistani authorities began an aggressive campaign to expel as many as possible of the Afghan refugees who had lived there for over forty years. Amid tensions over cross-border security and deteriorating relations between the Afghan and Pakistani governments, nearly 365,000 of the country's estimated 1.5 million documented refugees were coerced into returning to Afghanistan along with just over 220,000 of their nearly 1 million undocumented compatriots. The arrest and public humiliation of Sharbat Gula was regarded by many observers as a cynical attempt to publicise this hard-line policy.

The years since her 2002 moment in the spotlight had not been kind to Sharbat Gula. Having profited handsomely from her childhood photograph and the post-9/11 story of her rediscovery, *National Geographic* had set up a fund to benefit Afghan children as well as arranging for a stipend to be paid to Sharbat Gula herself. However, as the *Guardian* reported after her arrest, there were claims that little of the money had reached her. Her husband and one of her adult daughters had died of hepatitis B, a disease with which she too had been diagnosed. She now faced the possibility of fourteen years of imprisonment for the crime of obtaining false documents in order to enrol her children in school and sell her house.

However, after Steve McCurry and *National Geographic* joined the international furore about her arrest, Gula pleaded guilty to the charges against her and was sentenced to a fine of 110,000 rupees. The provincial governor then offered to allow her to remain in the country but, humiliated by the fifteen days she had spent in prison, she instead opted to return to Afghanistan with her children. President Ashraf Ghani greeted them at a reception at the presidential palace in Kabul, where he handed Gula the keys to a home that was gifted to her by the government. *National Geographic* was reported to have arranged to pay for the family's medical bills.

A few weeks later, she reflected on her life and on the impact of her portrait in an interview with BBC World News. She talked about the hardship of displacement, her regret at having been married at the age of thirteen rather than completing her education, the harshness of her arrest and imprisonment and her happiness about her family's new life in Kabul. Of the photo that had captured her haunting green eyes, she said: 'The photo created more problems than benefits. It made me famous but also led to my imprisonment.' She added, however, that she was proud that the income from the photograph had helped a lot of widows and orphans and that she hoped to establish a foundation to undertake similar work herself.

Afghan girls like Sharbat Gula, like Aesha Mohammadzai, like Zoya as she stood onstage in New York waiting for Oprah Winfrey to unveil her, were rendered into icons of victimhood. As icons, they are expected to suffer in silence while others explain their condition and determine their fate. To do otherwise is to fail to conform to the requirements of the role. Fortunately, those who conscripted them into the role have a talent for not noticing this inconvenient lapse.

2

CANDLE IN THE WIND

#Malala is a shameful act which must be condemned,
but liberal fascists are using this for their own propa-
ganda.
> – Samia Raheel Qazi, Twitter, October 2012

A drone attack may kill two or three terrorists but it will
not kill terrorism. If the drones continue terrorism will
spread.
> – Malala Yousafzai

Raheel Qazi was nothing if not a persuasive politician. If
she had not yet convinced the entire female population of
Pakistan to sign up for the Halq-e-Khawateen, the women's
wing of the Jamaat-e-Islami (JI), she had managed to
convince my daughter that there could be no more exciting
way to celebrate her eighth birthday than to attend an

Islamist mass wedding in the North West Frontier Province (now known as Khyber Pakhtunkhwa). It would be a party, Qazi assured her – a huge event with more than 150 brides. We should get dressed up in our best clothes and all our jewellery.

I had expected that my daughter would be bored during my interviews with the JI, so I was stunned when afterwards she named Raheel Qazi and her nine-year-old daughter as 'two of my favourite people in Pakistan'. I mentally replayed the interview: Qazi and I had talked, while Qazi's daughter had sat at our feet and sliced apples and guavas for us. The little girl was very attractive – huge green eyes framed by a spotless hijab. She looked serious and lovely – I could understand why my daughter might want to be like her. And Qazi herself had won her heart by asking her, 'When you grow up, will you become a warrior for Islam?' I had thought that I was raising my daughter to be proud of her Muslim identity, but in Pakistan I realised that from my daughter's perspective, I seemed to be constantly apologising. 'We are Muslim, but not *that* kind of Muslim.' My daughter had experienced very little direct Islamophobia, but she was aware of the constant flow of negative media and political commentary and, at seven years old, she was already sick of it. And, of course, the appeal of an Islam that refuses to apologise for itself is not limited to seven-year-olds.

That was in 2004. Seven years later, a young woman almost exactly the same age as my daughter was to have a less happy encounter with Raheel Qazi. Malala Yousafzai had become a symbol of female entitlement to education in the face of the 2009 Taliban edict ordering the closure of private girls' schools in the Swat district where they had taken control. As the twelve-year-old daughter of a local school principal, she wrote a blog under the name 'Gul Makai' for the BBC Urdu website, later translated into English as 'Diary of a Pakistani schoolgirl'. Her series of short entries described her determination to continue her education despite the Taliban's closure of schools in her area. Later that year, she starred in a *New York Times* documentary and her identity as the BBC schoolgirl blogger was revealed. Now a public figure, she met with high-profile national and international figures and was awarded Pakistan's first National Youth Peace Prize. But, of course, her defiance won her enemies as well as praise. In October 2012, Taliban gunmen boarded the bus on which she was returning to school, singled her out by name, and shot her through the head. Two of her classmates were also injured in the shooting.

The attack on Malala caused national and international shockwaves but soon generated a backlash against her within Pakistan as the initial surge in support for her dissolved into a melee of double-thinking and conspiracy theories. And, as Malala wrote in her memoir *I Am Malala*, Qazi was among the most vocal of those who turned on her in the days after the shooting. 'She called me an American stooge and showed a photograph of me sitting next to Ambassador Richard Holbrooke as evidence of me "hobnobbing with US military authority"!'

Raheel Qazi's reaction to the shooting of Malala ought not to have surprised me. I had always found it hard to reconcile her personal charm with her political outlook and, in particular, her support for the notorious Hudood Ordinances – laws introduced in 1979 as part of President Zia-ul-Haq's programme of 'Islamisation' – under which thousands of women have been jailed for real or alleged adultery. And her hostility to Malala was not particularly exceptional in Pakistan – or among Pakistanis living in the West, for that matter. Nonetheless, I was horrified. Raheel Qazi was an educated and articulate woman. How could she respond so dismissively to the attempted murder of a fifteen-year-old girl?

But the cause that Malala had championed – the right of women and girls to education – has been cited by the United States as one of the primary justifications for the War on Terror. This war has plunged Pakistan into a state of apparently permanent crisis. In particular, the campaign undertaken by the United States against alleged 'high-value militants' in Pakistan's north since 2004 has driven Pakistanis to close ranks against external criticism. Although only a small proportion of Pakistanis live in the affected areas, the secrecy surrounding the campaign and conflicting information about the number of civilian casualties has generated anti-American hostility throughout the country. A Pew research poll found that the number of Pakistanis who regard the United States as an enemy had risen from 69 per cent to 74 per cent in the years between 2009 and 2012. And this anger is directed not only towards America itself, but towards anyone who is suspected of collusion – even a teenage girl.

Women and Feminism in Pakistan

The emergence of female Islamism comes as a disruption to the established understanding of the role of women in Pakistani politics. This story usually opens with their role in the foundation of the state of Pakistan in 1947 before describing the ways in which women worked within the system to campaign for the modernisation of gender norms under both civilian and military governments during the early post-Independence decades – an era that came to an abrupt end with the rise to power of General Zia-ul-Haq in 1977.

General Zia-ul-Haq caused widespread international shock by overthrowing and later executing his elected (if autocratic and corrupt) predecessor, Zulfikar Ali Bhutto, in 1977. But, after the 1979 Soviet invasion of Afghanistan, the United States' strategic interest in forming an alliance with a front-line state outweighed its stated commitment to liberal democracy and human rights. Pakistan became a major recipient of US military aid, as well as the conduit through which weapons were conveyed to the anti-Soviet Afghan *mujahideen*.

The role played by JI in this process, particularly its working relationship with the military, bestowed the party with a degree of power that far exceeded its modest level of electoral support. President Zia-ul-Haq sought political legitimacy through a programme of Islamisation whose primary consequence was to render more vulnerable the lives of Pakistani women. According to a famous slogan of the time, their proper place was circumscribed by the *chador aur char diwari* (the veil and four walls [of the home]) – and resistance to that message placed the women's movement, led by the Women's Action Forum, at the forefront of the movement for the restoration of democracy. Violent confrontations between women activists and the police became a potent symbol of the struggle against dictatorship.

The central feminist issue became the imperative to oppose the Islamisation of the political and legal systems, and in particular to campaign for the repeal of the Hudood Ordinances. Under the Law of Evidence, a woman's testimony was held to be worth only half that of a man's. Prosecutions for *zina* (fornication) fell particularly heavily upon women, including rape victims, with the issue of consent considered irrelevant. Since pregnancy provides hard evidence of sexual activity, women who had become pregnant without a licit sexual partner could be prosecuted for *zina* while the men who impregnated them, often forcibly, escaped punishment.

The Soviet withdrawal from Afghanistan in 1988 and the death of Zia-ul-Haq in a plane crash in the same year raised hopes for social and particularly legal reforms that would enhance the status of Pakistani women. However, the return to civilian government (even under a glamorous female prime minister in the form of Benazir Bhutto) did not reverse the erosion of women's legal standing. Neither Bhutto nor her rival and successor, Nawaz Sharif, had the political will to overturn the Hudood Ordinances. And the corruption and ineffectualness of their governments throughout the 1990s sapped popular enthusiasm for civilian rule. In 1999, the military again took direct control with the seizure of power by General (later President) Pervez Musharraf.

Like Afghanistan, Pakistan had fallen off the international radar during the 1990s, but in the wake of the 9/11 attacks in New York and Washington, and the subsequent launching of Operation Enduring Freedom by the United States in Afghanistan, it was once again a front-line state and a (supposed) valued ally of the United States. Musharraf declared that he would implement a policy of 'enlightened moderation' in the face of religious extremism. In 2006, he introduced the Women's Protection Act to alleviate the consequences of the Hudood Ordinances through procedural changes, such as bringing rape charges under regular criminal rather than sharia law and requiring that complaints of *zina* be filed before a court rather than with the police (a move intended to discourage false complaints). However, the Ordinances themselves remain in place.

Moreover, the post-9/11 era has seen Islamisation, in the form of religious nationalism, permeate Pakistani public space to an unprecedented degree. The oppression of women committed by the state and the legal system has come to be overshadowed by systemic extra-judicial violence committed by non-state actors, ranging from beatings and murders of women accused of sexual and 'moral' transgressions to the killing of female health workers. And this era has also seen a rising number of accounts of Pakistani women as Islamist combatants and enforcers rather than its victims. In contrast to the era of Zia-ul-Haq, when Islamisation was experienced as an imposition upon women by patriarchal men, recent shifts in Islamist cultural and political attitudes and practices are at least in part being generated and reinforced by women themselves. This last development has caused significant discord and angst among Pakistani feminists and scholars, as has been discussed by activists and researchers such as Nazish Brohi and sociologist Amina Jamal.

Jamaat-e-Islami

I was first introduced to the Jamaat-e-Islami women by a member of a non-religious NGO, the Aurat Foundation. Given its focus on women's rights, I was surprised to be told that the Aurat Foundation had a cordial working relationship with the JI women. But the Aurat Foundation runs a training programme and outreach programme for women in order to encourage their participation in politics. Through this programme they have dealings with women of a whole range of political affiliations, including the JI.

The Jamaat-e-Islami was founded in 1941 by Maulana Abul Ala Maududi (1903–1979) who, alongside Hassan al-Banna and Sayyid Qutb, ranks among the most prominent twentieth-century Islamist thinkers. Maududi was an important influence on Islamist movements worldwide, in particular the Egyptian Muslim Brotherhood and its martyred leader Sayyid Qutb.

After Pakistan's Independence, Maududi campaigned for the transformation of the new nation into an Islamic state, not simply a state for Muslims in which religion would be a purely personal matter. For Maududi, Islam was a complete social system that provided an alternative to the failings of both Western liberalism and Soviet communism. In an Islamic state, sovereignty belonged to God and His will as expressed through sharia should be the source of all law (criminal, civil and constitutional). The failure to adequately implement sharia was, he claimed, responsible for the failure of Islam to withstand the ravages of European colonialism.

On gender issues, Maududi cited the mistreatment of women as a feature of backward, primitive societies. As a community progresses:

> it begins to realize that it cannot go any further by keeping half of its population in a state of bondage. Thus, when the community finds the pace of advancement being retarded, the feeling of necessity compels it to enable the neglected half also to keep pace with the advanced half.

Unfortunately, many communities then overcompensate, choosing to 'bestow undue freedom upon the fair sex with the result that the latter's excessive freedom deals a fatal blow at the family life which is the very basis of civilization'.

In contrast, Maududi advocated strict purdah (gender segregation) and veiling. Men, he claimed, are not to be trusted with the sight of unrelated women – although women, having greater self-control, may be allowed to watch men. Such measures were necessary because:

> the free intermingling of the sexes brings in its wake a flood of obscenity, licentiousness and sexual perversion,

which ruin the morals of the whole community. Along with this moral depravity starts the gradual weakening of the intellectual, physical and material energies of the community, which eventually leads it to total collapse and destruction.

In practice, however, Maududi's attitudes to gender issues were more pragmatic than this fulminating would suggest. His opposition to the regime of General Ayub Khan led him to support the political candidacy of Fatima Jinnah, despite his endorsement of female seclusion and his previous criticism of Jinnah herself for her violation of purdah. And during the 1970s, as discussed in the writings of researcher Amina Jamal, he set about actively mobilising women so that the party could take advantage of parliamentary seats that had been reserved for female candidates. However, when the Pakistan People's Party tried to establish an alliance with the JI during the final years of the Sharif government in 1993, the JI refused to co-operate unless Benazir Bhutto and her mother were removed from leadership positions.

Guarding Muslim Women's Rights

Despite its well-earned reputation for aggressive misogyny, JI has had an active women's wing since 1948. This organisation plays a highly symbolic role by asserting that, far from oppressing women, Islam (as represented by their organisation) protects them from the disintegration of their families and the commercial exploitation of their bodies. Rather than envying Western women, they see them as oppressed by a society rife with divorce, family breakdown and sexualised media. Worse still, Western cultural and political imperialism, in the name of women's rights, threatens to subject Muslim women to similar levels of degradation.

My first encounter with Raheel Qazi and other Jamaat-e-Islami women was at a 2000 forum for which women members from the major Pakistani political parties and non-government organisations were invited to Mansoora, the Jamaat-e-Islami's model township outside Lahore. Mansoora provides schools, mosques, medical facilities, visitors' accommodation and residential housing for party members and their families. Once you get past the security at the entrance (never in my experience a straightforward exercise) it is a quiet, pleasant environment with bougainvillea spilling over walled courtyards and children playing on the streets.

The most senior JI woman present swept regally towards me, bestowing a beatific smile. 'I am Raheel Qazi,' she announced, and embraced me. Her status was clear by her manner, despite her plain though smart clothes and the fact that she lacked most of the gold jewellery commonly worn by those Pakistani women who can afford it. The JI frowns on ostentatious ornamentation, and in fact Qazi did not need it to establish her rank. Her father, Qazi Hussain Ahmad, was the party's emir, and she herself holds a senior position in the women's wing (at that time, head of the international relations and political department). Her name, if not her face (which is always veiled in mixed-gender settings and in photographs), is well known.

I chatted informally for a while with other JI women, all of them educated professionals. They were likeable and articulate – in my notes, I wrote 'need to remind self that charm is not a measure of political morality'. But the charm worked. My preconceptions of them as devoid of personality, humour and intelligence – a breed of Islamist Stepford Wives – fell away fast. I was not persuaded by their ideology, but I did find myself enjoying their company. I had a stimulating conversation about the importance of female education with the principal of the Mansoora girls' school, not unlike a conversation that I might have had with a colleague in Australia. I was reminded of where I was by another woman, who denounced the tactics of secular women's organisations – one improved the lives of women through education (especially education in Islamic studies), not through 'holding demonstrations and getting into fights'. Presumably she was objecting to the ideology of the demonstrations, rather than the mere act of demonstrating. The JI women's wing has held public demonstrations on issues including the French ban on headscarves in state schools, the US military intervention in Afghanistan, the murder of MMA activists in Karachi, 'vulgarity being spread through the media, under the aegis of the government', the Indian occupation of Kashmir, the alleged desecration of the Holy Qur'an by US guards in Guantanamo Bay, the publication of the infamous 'Danish cartoons', and in support of the Hudood Ordinances.

The forum commenced; Qazi was the main speaker. She had invited everybody to gather at Mansoora, she said, because Pakistan faced a challenge to its very survival.

Globalisation threatened Islam; Muslims had to unite to reject Western cultural and media invasion. In the face of such a threat, it was necessary for women of all political persuasions to come together for the good of the nation. At one stage, she and the other JI women present pinned their niqabs across their faces in order to allow a group of male photographers to be admitted. Qazi's charisma beamed straight through her niqab, but she removed it again for her female audience once the photographers had left.

After the forum, Qazi agreed to an interview to discuss her organisation's work and the issues confronting women in Pakistan. In particular, she contrasted her approach with that of the 'elitist' secular women's rights groups who had been fighting for years to have the Hudood Ordinances overturned. Such women were only interested in 'blackening Pakistan's name', not in truly working for the uplift of women. They had adopted a 'Western' concept of women's rights, which was hostile to Islam and which failed to acknowledge that Muslim women had been granted all the rights they needed from the very earliest days of the religion. She (Qazi) and her colleagues in the JI were far more representative of ordinary Pakistani women than were the women of the secular women's rights groups, who were running a foreign agenda funded by foreign money.

The Hudood Ordinances could not be overturned because they were not man-made laws – they were the law of Islam and accepted as such by the vast majority of Pakistani women. She was able to concede (or, rather, appear to concede) a certain amount of ground without deviating from the party line. Yes, there were innocent women languishing in Pakistani jails, charged with *zina* (illicit sex), although the numbers were not as high as 'certain groups' claimed. However, the problem lay not in the law itself, but in its implementation. She cited the fact that neither marriages nor divorces are commonly registered in rural areas of Pakistan, so that a woman may believe herself to be legally divorced and remarried, only to have her first husband claim that she is still married to him, and so guilty of *zina* with her second husband. She also noted the problem of police corruption, which allowed those engaged in personal feuds to have their enemies charged with crimes, including crimes under the Hudood Ordinances. These were problems that could be solved without reform or repeal of the Ordinances themselves, simply by improving the processes by which the current laws were implemented. And, she correctly noted, problems such as police corruption and the glacial slowness of the legal system were not specific to the Ordinances, but applied to the implementation of Pakistani law as a whole.

She also described the work that the JI women were undertaking through their welfare organisations, the Women's Aid Trust and Al Khidmat, to alleviate the suffering of women who had been charged under the Hudood Ordinances. They provided legal advice and support to women in jail and Qazi spoke passionately about the unfounded accusations against some of their clients. However, she blamed these injustices on the malicious conduct of those who had made false allegations rather than on any flaw in the Ordinances themselves.

Qazi also denounced the oppression of Pakistani women by non-Islamic cultural practices, such as honour killing. According to feminist organisations such as the Aurat Foundation, hundreds of Pakistani women die every year in such killings, murdered by their families in order to regain the honour destroyed when women allegedly engage in adultery, marry outside of their community or without parental consent, or fall victim to rape. This practice, Qazi declared, was 'completely unIslamic' and should be eliminated (although, again, she referred to the exploitation of the honour killing issue by those hostile to Pakistan and Islam). Her denunciation was so passionate, and so apparently unqualified, that it was only later that I realised I had not questioned her on the most central legal issue concerning honour killing: the Qisas (retribution) and Diyat (blood money) Ordinance. Under this ordinance, the family of a murder victim could choose to waive the penalty for the crime, with or without the payment of blood money. This had obvious repercussions in the case of honour killings, where the murderer belongs to the same family as the victim, effectively allowing men to kill their female relatives with impunity. The JI has opposed all attempts to reform or abolish the Qisas and Diyat Ordinance, which it claims is derived from Qur'anic injunctions and so beyond the reach of human decision making. My failure to quiz Qazi on this point had no substantial impact on my research. Her opinion (which was in line with that of her party) was on the public record. I was nonetheless mortified by the oversight: Qazi, I reflected ruefully, must have thought me a pushover. We parted on friendly terms, Qazi bestowing another beatific smile and two beautifully gift-wrapped volumes of essays by Maududi – as I was to discover, the standard JI gift for visitors.

The threat of a slide into 'Western' moral and family breakdown is used by JI, including its women's wing, to justify the disciplining of Pakistani women to ensure that they stay within Islamic boundaries. Pakistani feminists are represented as proxies of the Westernising agenda. As such, they are not only accused of facilitating the spread of Western social and sexual norms, they are also seen as agents of US foreign policy, since a decline in Islamic standards would undermine the country's entire *raison d'être* and endanger its physical survival. Discussion among the JI women flowed freely between gender and foreign policy issues, with clear links drawn between the two. Transnational feminist activism, then, is represented as a form of political as well as religious treason, while the JI women's role as guardians of Islamic social norms is not only a religious duty but a matter of national security.

A few weeks after 9/11, I returned to Mansoora in the hope of another meeting with Raheel Qazi. I had not been able to contact her prior to trekking out from Lahore, so the security guard at the gate directed me to a book-lined office for an initial meeting with one of the male leaders. A map of the world in the background showed the Muslim-majority countries in shades of green and the non-Muslim countries in red, the depth of colour indicating the proportion of the population that was Muslim. Pakistan was shaded deep green; Australia was an appropriate Uluru ochre.

The JI men had always been more assiduous than the women in establishing my credentials and allegiances, and the lull between the fall of the Twin Towers and the outbreak of the shooting war in Afghanistan was not an opportune time to turn up at Mansoora without an appointment. I comprehensively flunked an on-the-spot Q&A on Islam – the JI's brand of Islam in particular – and was relieved to be able to provide the answer to the final question.

'Do you know what your name means?'

'Yes, of course. It means grateful.'

Fail. 'It does not mean grateful to just anyone. It means grateful to Allah.'

A phone call came through with the news that Maulana Fazl ur Rahman, the leader of the Jamiat Ulema-e-Islam (JUI), Pakistan's other major Islamist party, had been placed under arrest. I was ushered out through the door and in the direction of Raheel Qazi's home with a pile of new-edition books by Maududi to add to my growing collection. These particular books, I was told, were 'suitable for Muslims who have strayed from the true path'. They were heavy and cumbersome, but it did not seem tactful to refuse them.

Raheel Qazi greeted me with a hug and sat me down on a sofa with cups of tea and a bowl of pistachios before us. She seemed far less on edge than her colleague had been, although I had thought that she would have greater cause for personal concern. I commented sympathetically that she must be worried about her father, after the arrest of Fazl ur Rahman. She reproved me. 'No, sister, I am not worried, because I put my trust in Allah. Whatever may happen is His will, and I do not fear it.' Her own husband had recently died, but this, too, was Allah's will. She gestured towards her own primary school-aged daughter.

'She goes to a big Islamic school. It has 1,000 students and Osama is a hero to them all. Well, this attitude is very popular among the young.' Like most Pakistanis at the time, Qazi herself refused to believe that bin Laden was responsible for the attacks in New York and Washington and was fiercely opposed to the pending US-led military intervention in Afghanistan. The appropriate way to deal with the Taliban's treatment of women was education. As she pointed out, '"Talib" means "student"':

> They are students, they don't understand what is Islamic and what is not. We don't need to bomb them for that. We need to educate them about Islam and to help them rebuild society. Afghanistan has had so many years of war – they don't have the resources to build girls' schools.

She updated me on the offerings of the JI's educational programme for girls, which she said provided its students with the most up-to-date modern knowledge in an appropriately Islamic environment. They also offered self-defence classes – of course, in an all-female environment. Such healthy and enjoyable exercise, and in these times . . .

She may have just been referring to rising crime levels, of course. But I took her to mean the battalions of US soldiers who stood ready to invade Afghanistan and from there march through the Khyber Pass to defile Pakistani womanhood.

The 2002 elections saw a backlash against President Musharraf's alliance with the United States. Support for the Jamaat-e-Islami reached an all-time high-water mark, with the Muttahida Majlis-e-Amal (MMA) alliance, of which it was a member, gaining one quarter of the share of the vote for the National Assembly and taking power in the North West Frontier Province. The new parliament included a quota of reserved seats for women, with candidates to be appointed by the parties based on their share of the vote. The Jamaat-e-Islami had opposed the introduction of the quotas but nonetheless nominated members of its women's wing to take their place in parliament. Raheel Qazi was among the new members of the National Assembly, a role which she was reported as explaining as a regrettable necessity forced on her by the introduction of gender quotas: 'the party requires women to sit in the assembly for numbers. Otherwise, we are only here to create human beings, not governments.'

And so in 2004 I returned with my daughter in tow to see Qazi in her new role as a parliamentarian. I asked her who looked after her own children while she was away from home and she assured me that they were well cared for in her absence. Various relatives lived in Mansoora and, anyway, 'the whole of Mansoora is a family'. Her work was arduous and required extensive travel, but there was never any shortage of people to help out.

In a dark premonition of the Taliban's later attacks on female education in Pakistan, several girls' schools had recently been torched in the North West Frontier Province, where Qazi's party was in government. Qazi claimed that these attacks were nothing more than a conspiracy to smear the provincial government. The MMA was absolutely in support of both basic and higher education for girls – Islamic education of course. This put them in conflict with the national government, which was guilty of allowing Pakistani education to be influenced by the United States and by foreign-funded NGOs, who wanted to take the Qur'an out of the science curriculum.

The wedding to which Qazi had invited my daughter and me was an example of the support that her party provided to women and girls. Marriages in Pakistan are a crushing expense for many families, with daughters left unmarried because their parents are unable to cover the cost of their dowries, not to mention the wedding itself. Hosting the mass wedding ceremony and providing the brides with a dowry box would relieve the families of this burden and provide their daughters with the opportunity to enter matrimony. Qazi's father would preside over the ceremony himself.

And so my daughter and I found ourselves in a field outside Nowshera in the North West Frontier Province, where the JI had erected two huge marquees in order to accommodate the gender-segregated event. Inside the women's marquee, the guests removed their niqabs and burqas and prepared to celebrate. The brides sat onstage in a line, their finery displayed to full effect. I was introduced to one of them, an articulate high school student who explained that she would continue to live with her parents until she had completed her education – she planned to become a doctor – but that she was happy to have the security and status of a married woman. Her husband's family fully supported her plans for her education and her career. I asked one of the older women whether the JI would help to ensure that this promise was kept and was assured that of course they would. The JI had great respect for educated women.

Life in the Drone-Attack Zone

The US campaign of 'targeted assassination' by drone attack in Pakistan began with little fanfare under the Bush presidency in 2004. Bush's successor, Barack Obama, escalated the programme by authorising 'signature strikes' against not only known individuals but those who 'bear certain signatures, or defining characteristics associated with terrorist activity, but whose identities aren't known'. Information about the impact of this campaign is difficult and dangerous to obtain. The target zone is the Federally Administered Tribal Areas (FATA) region of north-western Pakistan, which is closed to foreigners and to Pakistanis from outside the region unless accompanied by a military escort. In Washington, too, information about the process by which its targets are selected remains a closely guarded secret. According to some reports, all males of fighting age killed in drone attacks are classified as terrorists by the Pentagon, unless and until other information comes to light. Unsurprisingly, the numbers of civilian casualties caused by drone attacks are deeply contested.

One of those most closely involved in gathering data about the impact of drone strikes in Pakistan is the

Islamabad-based lawyer Shahzad Akbar, who has sought compensation on victims' behalf from both the Pakistani and the United States governments. Akbar described this campaign to me during his 2013 visit to Australia, during which he alleged that Australia could be in breach of international law if the joint Australian–US defence facility at Pine Gap was found to be involved in identifying targets for attack. (Pine Gap's role was eventually confirmed in documents from the US National Security Agency, leaked by whistleblower Edward Snowden.)

Shahzad Akbar has collated information from his clients that paints a picture of communities living with the stress of constant surveillance and the fear that death could strike at any time:

> It's a very abnormal life at the moment because the area is literally cordoned off by the Pakistan military. On top of that, they're living under constant surveillance from the drones. In some of the concentrated areas of attack, people limit their movements because of the fear of being killed or maimed. They don't go out in bigger groups because they don't dare go out in groups of more than three or four. They don't go out to weddings, mosques, they don't send their kids to school any more because of the fear of drones.

Akbar's claims are validated by a 2012 report from the Stanford International Human Rights and Conflict Resolution Clinic which documents the impact of drone attacks in North Waziristan, not only in terms of casualties but also in terms of their impact on the broader family networks and communities involved. According to the report, fear of drone attacks has led parents to withdraw their children from school both because large gatherings of people have been the targets of attack and because the level of uncertainty leads them to believe that there is no point in preparing their offspring for future careers.

Some of those injured in strikes reported reduced access to education and desire to learn because of the physical, emotional and financial impacts of the strikes; some families have pulled their children out of school to take care of injured relatives or to compensate for the income lost after the death or injury of a relative; while others reported keeping their children at home due to fear that they would be killed in a drone strike.

Like Malala, Sadaullah Wazir was a fourteen-year-old high school student when violence threw his life into turmoil. However, the violence that cost him an eye and both legs was inflicted not by a Taliban attack, but by a US drone strike. 'Before the drone strikes started, my life was very good. I used to go to school and I used to be quite busy with that, but after the drone strikes, I stopped going to school now. I was happy because I thought I would become a doctor,' Sadaullah told Akbar. 'Two missiles [were] fired at our hujra (guest-house) and three people died. My cousin and I were injured. We didn't hear the missile at all and then it was there.' As Akbar relates, Sadaullah died in 2012 without ever receiving justice.

Despite his work on behalf of victims like Sadaullah, Shahzad Akbar told me that he personally did not share the anti-American sentiment that is running at high levels in Pakistan:

> It's a matter of being critical, of investigating the war on terror in Afghanistan and Pakistan and challenging the axis of power. If you are the most powerful nation on earth and a nation that claims to represent due process and rule of law, then you can't just go around the world killing people without due process just because it's too easy.

Malala, Schoolgirl and Symbol

In claiming responsibility for the attack on Malala, the Tehrik-i-Taliban (TTP) stated: 'If anyone thinks that Malala was targeted because of education, that is absolutely wrong, and propaganda of the media. Malala was targeted because of her pioneer role in preaching secularism and so-called enlightened moderation. And whomsoever commit so in future too will be targeted again by TTP.'

Angelina Jolie wrote an article a few days later titled 'We are all Malala', Madonna stripped down to her bra and G-string to reveal a fake 'MALALA' tattoo across her back at a concert on the evening after the attack, while Laura Bush, in a column in the *Washington Post* that week, compared her to Anne Frank. In Pakistan, too, the initial response was overwhelming support for Malala, with figures from across the political spectrum condemning her attackers and hundreds of people lining up to donate blood at the hospital where she and her classmates were being treated. However, this consensus quickly fragmented into a melee of double-thinking and cognitive dissonance.

Despite the Taliban's explicit claim of responsibility, many Pakistanis refused to believe Malala's attackers originated within their country and instead blamed a CIA and/or Zionist plot to defame Pakistan and justify drone attacks. An op-ed by Dr Shahida Wizarat in the *Frontier Post*, which claimed to detect CIA 'footprints' on the shooting of Malala, stated:

> It is also intriguing to note after the attack on Malala Yousafzai the casualties from drone attacks increased to 18 and 27 the day before and yesterday respectively. This precious loss of life and the crimes against humanity committed by the US against these innocents is now not drawing any attention in the international media.

Cricket legend-turned-politician Imran Khan exemplified this line of thinking, visiting Malala in hospital and offering to cover her medical expenses. However, at a press conference, 'Taliban Khan' (as some media dubbed him) repeatedly declined to name her attackers, later citing his commitment to a political solution and his concern for the safety of party workers.

In the midst of this blame-shifting, Raheel Qazi tweeted a photograph of Malala and her father attending a meeting with Richard Holbrooke, the United States Special Representative for Afghanistan and Pakistan. Posted at a time when Malala was still fighting for her life, Qazi's tweet described the photograph as showing 'Malala amreeki fauji hukkkam k sath' (Malala with the leaders of the American army), and was tagged to a number of prominent journalists. Qazi's words and her circulation of that image attracted widespread condemnation from Pakistan's liberal voices for its attempt to displace responsibility for the attempted murder and for its depiction of Malala as having consorted with the enemy. Journalist Beena Sarwar tweeted 'Daughter @sraqazi of ex JI chief implies it's ok to shoot #malala – a new low – even for the JI'.

Qazi proclaimed her sympathy for Malala and her condemnation of the attack in subsequent tweets and television interviews, but maintained her displacement of responsibility. 'Attack on Malala Yousafzai is deplorable and I strongly condemn this act. May Allah recover her soon.' '#Malala is a shameful act which must be condemned, but liberal fascists are using this for their own propaganda.' Another tweet provided a presumably unintentional echo of Elton John's tributes to the late Marilyn Monroe and Princess Diana: '#malala May u live long. Get well soon dear candle in the wind.'

For some of Malala's supporters, on the other hand, the shooting raised difficult questions about whether she could have been better protected by those who had profited from her courage. Irfan Ashraf, the Pakistani journalist who had helped to produce the documentary 'Class Dismissed', which profiled Malala for the *New York Times* wrote afterwards that he regarded himself as having contributed to the series of events that almost cost Malala her life. He posed the question, 'Would media professionals in the West put their own children in the path of harm the way they have allowed themselves to do with children in poor countries?'

A month after the attack on Malala, Taliban violence encroached on Raheel Qazi's own family life when a burqa-clad suicide bomber targeted her father's convoy during a visit to Pakistan's Federally Administered Tribal Areas. According to media reports, the attack on the Jamaat-e-Islami's former emir (Ahmed had retired as leader in 2008 after almost a decade at the helm) was retaliation for his comments in a television interview a few months earlier in which he had said that 'the Afghan Taliban's resistance against US-led coalition forces in Afghanistan is true jihad, but that of the Pakistani Taliban in Pakistan is unIslamic'. Pakistani Taliban leader Hakimullah Mehsud responded with a video message describing Qazi Hussain Ahmed as 'a traitor to the cause of jihad and a secret member of the Jewish lobby'. Ahmed declined to comment on Hakimullah's video-tape, beyond confirming that he knew of its existence.

Ahmed was uninjured in the attack upon his convoy, which left three men injured and the female bomber dead. However, a few months later he died of cardiac arrest. In a cover story headlined 'Saint Qazi', *Newsweek Pakistan* speculated that he may have succumbed to stress following the attempt on his life. The obituary described him as a moderating force in Pakistani's Islamist politics, noting his various attempts to end sectarian violence, his flexible attitude towards his enemies and his fondness for quoting the verses of Iqbal, Pakistan's national poet. But, just as Ahmed had blamed the 'cowardly' attempt on Malala's life on 'nefarious designs' to justify military intervention in the tribal areas, he declined to blame the Taliban for the attempt on his own life, instead attributing it to an anti-Pakistan conspiracy between the US, India and Israel.

Nobel: Repercussions at Home

In 2014, just a couple of days after Malala became the youngest-ever recipient of the Nobel Peace Prize, I returned to Mansoora to catch up with Raheel Qazi. Malala had not become any more popular in Pakistan in the years since she was shot. She was vilified as an attention seeker and an opportunist, with those who defended her online slammed with the label 'BC' – *behanchud* (sister fucker). Her memoir (co-authored with British journalist Christina Lamb) was banned by two associations of Pakistani private schools who labelled her 'a tool in the hands of the Western powers'. As the television in the foyer of my hotel broadcast the news of the youngest ever Nobel prize winner, a stylishly dressed young woman rolled her eyes dismissively. 'Why isn't she in Pakistan?'

It had been a decade since I had visited Mansoora, and the contact details I had for the women I'd met all those years ago were long since out of date. I had to spend a couple of long sessions talking with bearded men and waiting around in offices before I was escorted to the women's area for my meeting with Raheel Qazi.

Qazi was as hospitable as ever, sending for food and drinks and apologising for the time I'd spent waiting for her. We exchanged updates about our families, Qazi telling me that her daughter was in medical school and engaged to be married. I offered my condolences on the death of her father. Qazi thanked me and described Qazi Hussein as having had a very modern outlook. He had asked her permission before arranging her marriage – 'a revolutionary step' in their highly traditional family. 'I belong to a very orthodox family from the Pakhtoon culture. We are from the same province as Malala Yousafzai. It is a very restrictive province.'

'Of course, Malala has just been awarded the Nobel Peace Prize,' I noted.

'Yes, I congratulate her.'

'But her success has been controversial,' I observed.

Qazi agreed:

Still it is controversial because in Pakistan they don't believe it is for what she did for education or for any other reasons. They are asking what is the main reason. It is cosmetic. She is the daughter of the nation and we are proud of her, that she won the Nobel prize, but at the same time most Pakistanis are asking 'What is the special thing for Malala?'

Personally I have no clash with Malala – she is like my daughter, yes? And she wrote about me in her book – that I opposed her. I don't oppose her. I opposed the ideology in which the daughter of the nation ... they took her abroad and they symbolised her as a secular face of Pakistan. There is no chance for secularism in this country because it is 97 per cent Muslim.

A few days later, I interviewed theatre director Shaheed Nadeem. Nadeem's play *Burqavaganza* was banned in Pakistan in 2010 after Raheel Qazi complained to the National Council for the Arts that the play promoted 'dangerous liberal and elitist ideas'. Qazi never saw the play herself, but the fact that it featured men and women dancing around in burqas was more than enough to arouse her suspicions:

> The play itself, I don't think it was offensive to any faith, any religion, any interpretation of the religion. It was a fun play, it was a satire on the double-standards in society and the cover-ups in society. It's done in a tongue-in-cheek, sometimes totally burlesque fashion. Let's see how the world would look if everyone wore burqa.
>
> But Samia Raheel Qazi had a political agenda and she was told by her friends in the Jamaat-e-Islami that this was a play which had made fun of the burqa and she immediately, without even contacting us, without even finding out or maybe coming to the performance, asking for a DVD, raised the matter in the Parliament. In a big way.

This was not Nadeem's first brush with the authorities. As he noted, 'Telling the truth and telling it plainly and bluntly has never been easy in Pakistan.' Under Zia-ul-Haq's regime, his theatre company had been forced to perform clandestinely and he had spent time in prison. 'Now there are other factors because of the war in Afghanistan and al-Qaeda. America is now enemy number one. And if you're talking about women's rights and human rights, people think you're fulfilling an American agenda' – as Pakistan's young Nobel Laureate had discovered.

Nadeem had been stunned by the intense anti-Malala sentiment among a group of young up-and-coming Pakistanis he had met during a recent trip to Washington. The group was visiting the United States as part of a cultural exchange for which 'they had been selected on merit and their work on the community and the society was taken into account'. He continued:

> I was interested to hear their impressions about the US – the good and the bad. During our conversation, I just mentioned the word 'Malala' and I was totally shocked. This was a group that had aspired to come to the US and mingle with Americans, so they must be people with liberal or open minds. But on the topic of Malala, most of them said things like 'Who knows if she was really shot or if it was all media gimmicks?'
>
> That's where I lost my cool and I really gave it to them. 'For God's sake, use your brains, if you have any! If you think that a girl your age has become internationally famous, this is not her fault. It is just a combination of circumstances and her own commitment and her own struggle.' I was very disappointed.
>
> The attack on Malala was not an accident. It was planned and it was targeted. And she recovered and she carried on with her struggles. We should be proud of her. Even if you think she doesn't deserve her rewards, there is no need to be so bitter about it.

But to many Pakistanis, this is a zero-sum game in which any support given to Malala is regarded as having come at the expense of the victims of drone attacks.

Return to Pakistan

In March 2018, Malala Yousafzai returned to Pakistan for the first time since her emergency evacuation from the country nine years earlier. By this time, Malala had finished high school and commenced a degree in philosophy, politics and economics at Oxford University – a landmark that was greeted with global acclaim. However, as noted by an article in *Pakistan Today*, Malala's Pakistani critics attributed her educational achievement to 'seemingly disparate concerns such as the Trump Administration and the revival of White Supremacism in the US'. However, Malala Yousafzai is a more complex figure than the reductive portraits of her as either a puppet of US imperialism or a heroine of liberal feminism would lead one to believe. As Pakistani acaemic Shenila Khoja-Moolji noted in a 2018 article for Al Jazeera, 'Malala has spoken out against drone strikes; she has critiqued Israel's state violence targeted at Palestinians; she has donated money to re-build schools in Gaza; she has spoken out against bombings in Afghanistan and atrocities in Kashmir; and raised her voice for the betterment of refugees.'

Malala's four-day visit to her home country was conducted under tight security, with then-Prime Minister Abbasi telling her: 'The entire world gave you honour and respect and Pakistan will [also] . . . It is your home. Now you are no longer an ordinary citizen, your security is our responsibility.' This was not the view of Kashif Mirza, the president of the All-Pakistan Private Schools Federation, whose institutes announced that they would mark Malala's return by observing an 'I am not Malala' day and instructing their teachers to wear black armbands. In her address on national television, however, Malala proclaimed that 'Today is the happiest day of my life, because I have returned to my home country.'

A few months after Malala's visit to Pakistan, the Taliban leader who had ordered her attempted assassination was himself killed in a US drone attack on his convoy in the Afghan city of Kundar, near the border with Pakistan. Mullah Fazlullah was responsible for many other atrocities including the 2014 attack on the Army High School in Peshawar in which over 130 students and teachers were killed. Yet most of the media coverage of his death focused on his attempted assassination of Malala. They did not, however, see fit to recall Malala's analysis of drone attacks during a 2013 meeting with then US President Barack Obama. 'A drone attack may kill two or three terrorists but it will not kill terrorism. If the drones continue terrorism will spread.'

Outside Pakistan, Malala became the object of an outpouring of pity and compassion that has not been afforded to other child casualties of the War on Terror. As Khoja-Moolji notes, the attack on her '[took] place outside the context of "legitimate" drone strikes, and its bodily dimension is visible as it is captured in public archives such as newspaper photographs'. Unlike the anonymous, faceless victims of drone attacks, Malala is lauded as a symbol of global girlhood, worthy of attention and compassion – even if her own opinion of drone attacks are less welcome than are her thoughts on the importance of education and her condemnation of the Taliban.

Predictably, Malala's much-acclaimed educational achievements and her role as a global campaigner for girls' education has drawn unwelcome attention from the West's own anti-feminists. In an article for the far-right *Breitbart News* headlined 'Sorry to be rude, but Malala Yousafzai is becoming a bit of a bore', Milo Yiannopoulos described Malala's message as 'the type of cultural Marxism that you would expect from the United Nations, where her father, Ziauddin, is a Special Advisor on Global Education'. For Yiannopoulos, Malala's decision to continue to wear a headscarf – 'the garb of her oppressors' – is 'a bit off'. In the mainstream media, the comment sections below articles about her achievements featured complaints about the cost to the British taxpayer of her education and healthcare (despite the fact that these expenses were covered by the Pakistani government). Britain may have provided Malala with a far safer and more welcoming environment than is currently available to her in Pakistan, but, so far as some of its citizens are concerned, she is just another unwanted Muslim immigrant.

3

SHIFTING PERCEPTIONS

Marianne has a naked breast because she is feeding the people! She is not veiled, because she is free! That is the republic!
– French Prime Minister Manuel Valls, August 2016

This woman who sees without being seen frustrates the coloniser.
                        – Frantz Fanon, 'Algeria Unveiled', 1959

Whenever I'd visualised a race riot, I'd always pictured shadowy figures shrouded by heavy clothing as they vented their rage in a gloomy inner-city landscape. But this was Australia. When these patriots decided to hold a riot in December 2005, they held it on Cronulla beach in southern Sydney, on a bright sunny day, in a location that could have served for the set of an archetypal Aussie soap opera. In fact,

Cronulla had provided the backdrop for Gabrielle Carey and Kathy Lette's classic 1979 coming-of-age novel *Puberty Blues*, and the 1981 film of the same name. This was the quintessential Australian landscape of leisure and relaxation, which the rioters claimed to be reconquering from alien invaders of 'Middle Eastern appearance'. It looked more like a festival than a riot, really – at least at the outset.

The text messages that had summoned the crowd to the beach that day became notorious in the wake of the riot:

> This Sunday every Aussie in the shire get down to North Cronulla to support the Leb and Wog bashing day. Bring your mates. Let's show them that this is our beach and they're never welcome.

The demonstration was triggered by a confrontation between lifeguards and young Middle Eastern men, as well as the alleged harassment of 'white' women by young Lebanese men on the beach. Defending 'our' women against 'their' men – the oldest *casus belli* in the world. And 'their' women were not exempt from the retaliation that was meted out on the beach that day. Like the men, they were spat on and abused and told to go back to where they came from. Reports in the next day's *Sydney Morning Herald* described how a bare-chested boy in boardshorts chased a hijab-wearing teenage girl down the sand dunes and triumphantly tore off her headscarf as a battlefield trophy.

In the aftermath of the display of masculinist rage at Cronulla, a young Muslim woman emerged as a symbol of post-riot reconciliation. Mecca LaaLaa wore a specially designed red and yellow burqini provided by the garment's creator, local designer Aheda Zanetti, in order to participate in the government-funded 'On the Same Wave' programme under which young people from diverse backgrounds were encouraged to train as lifesavers. The image of a burqini-clad LaaLaa running into the surf alongside her more scantily clad fellow lifeguards appeared in media outlets around the world and was a centrepiece of *The Australian* newspaper's 'Heart of the Nation' marketing campaign. This advertisement featured scenes from around the country to illustrate all that was best about Australia, opening with a group of young people, including LaaLaa, sitting on the beach dressed in the distinctive yellow and red attire of Surf Lifesaving Australia.

The story of reconciliation and healing as symbolised by the 'On the same wave' programme and Mecca LaaLaa in particular received national and international media coverage. For Australians who had been left shaken by the riots, the image of Mecca LaaLaa in her Surf Lifesaving burqini provided a welcome reassertion of their country's commitment to multicultural inclusion. Though the burqini was an obvious target for racist derision and abuse, Susie Khamis' assessment that it 'makes the Australian beach a far more inclusive, accommodating space' was a widely shared sentiment.

Eleven years after *The Australian* had featured Mecca LaaLaa in its 'Heart of the Nation' campaign, the newspaper turned its spotlight on her again. This time, however, it did not present her as a positive symbol of Australian nationhood. Rather, its front-page report expressed outrage that the Australian Department of Foreign Affairs and Trade (DFAT) had provided sponsorship for the 'Faith, Fashion, Fusion: Muslim Women's Style in Australia' exhibition (in which LaaLaa was a prominent feature) to hold showings in Malaysia and Indonesia after several years touring Australia. *The Australian* decried this as DFAT 'spending taxpayers' money pretending that Islamic dress is part of our cultural identity. It is not and never has been.' Other Newscorp outlets published similar reports, with former Prime Minister Tony Abbott quoted as saying that DFAT had shown 'a very unfortunate readiness to sell out mainstream Australia'.

The Australian's eviction of Mecca LaaLaa from the heart of the nation came in the wake of a short-lived attempt by several councils in France to ban the burqini from their beaches in response to the terrorist attack in Nice that killed eighty-four people on Bastille Day in 2016. The mayor of Cannes justified the ban on the grounds that the burqini was a symbol of extremism and was 'not respectful of good morals and secularism'. Photographs of four armed police forcing a woman on a beach in Nice to remove some of her clothing in order to conform to the new regulation were published by media outlets around the world. A few days later, the French Council of State (Conseil d'État) overturned the edict by the town of Villeneuve-Loubet on the grounds that it 'seriously and clearly illegally breached fundamental freedoms'. The other bans were also overturned over the following few weeks. However, the topic of burqini bans remained on the political agenda in France throughout the 2017 election and beyond, with Front National candidate Marine Le Pen and the eventual winning candidate Emmanuel Macron taking opposing stances for and against, while the socialist then-Prime Minister Manuel Valls declared that the garment represented 'an archaic view of women's position in society' which was 'not compatible with French values and the Republic'. The Republic, he declared, was represented by the 'barebreasted Marianne'.

Although Australian-Lebanese designer Aheda Zanetti's company had trademarked the names 'burqini' and 'burkini', the term has entered the global vocabulary as a generic term for modest swimwear. Zanetti's chosen brand name may have significantly enhanced her product's success, but also contributed to the level of hostility directed towards it. Although the garment itself does not resemble a burqa (in the form of either the Afghan-style shuttlecock burqa which attracted headlines as a symbol of Taliban oppression or the niqab-style face-veil as used in French discourse), the name itself is widely read as a provocative signifier of extremism rather than as light-hearted word play.

The rationale deployed in support of the burqini bans illustrates what law professor and civil rights policymaker Sahar Aziz describes as a shift from 'hijab as a symbol of oppression into a symbol of terrorism'. However, the backlash against the burqini in both France and Australia also illustrates the perception of the veil as a cultural as well as a security hazard. If the burqini were permitted to become an unremarkable feature on 'our' beaches, then 'Islamic dress' might indeed come to be regarded as representative of 'our' cultural identity. The case of the burqini illustrates differing attitudes to secularism and multicultural governance, but also the capacity for both fashion and racist moral panics to travel across borders.

As 'the Muslim question' has become an increasingly important issue in domestic as well as international politics in Europe, North America and Australia, Muslim women have come to be regarded as the accomplices rather than (or as well as) the victims of Muslim men. This revised view was further strengthened by reports of women and girls abandoning their homes and families in the West to become part of the so-called Islamic State in Syria and Iraq. Discussions about Muslim-minority communities might once have focused on Muslim women as victims of oppressive patriarchal practices imported from their countries of origin, but the focus has now broadened to represent Muslim women as Islamic fifth columnists within the West. Even Muslims living demonstrably law-abiding suburban lives are resented for the changes their presence brings to those suburbs. The situation of Muslim women within the West shares many resonances with that of their co-religionists in Muslim-majority societies, but is further complicated by tension between competing concerns about immigration, racism, multiculturalism and gender norms.

The first generation of post-war Muslim migrants to western Europe were mostly men who arrived as guest workers and in the expectation that they would eventually return to their countries of origin. Wives and children were therefore generally left behind. However, as Sara R. Farris points out, when the post-Second World War labour shortage waned during the 1970s and governments in northern Europe began to impose barriers to entry, migrants who had no wish to return began to bring their spouses and children to join them, for fear of permanent exclusion and separation. And governments sought to incorporate and control these new arrivals using mechanisms already in place as the legacy from previous religious conflicts. In France, the mode of governance has been *laïcité* (generally translated as 'secularism') or the exclusion of religion from the public space. The United Kingdom, Canada and Australia have instead settled for a form of multicultural governance that allows for plural identities – however uneasily those hybrid identities may operate in practice.

Hate Crimes Against Muslim Women

As Muslim communities in the West came under scrutiny in the wake of the 11 September 2001 attacks in New York and Washington, women wearing hijab and other forms of Islamic dress were the most visible and immediate targets for verbal and physical harassment and abuse. A 2004 report by the Australian Human Rights and Equal Opportunity Commission (HREOC) into hostility against Arab and Muslim Australians documented a heightened sense of fear among Muslim women after experiences such as being spat on, threatened and assaulted. Women regarded the forcible removal of headscarves by strangers in public places as particularly degrading – 'akin to rape', in the opinion of one respondent. At the same time as the United States and its allies were claiming to have rescued Muslim women from Taliban oppression in Afghanistan, Muslim women within the nations of the rescuers were being subjected to less violent but nonetheless humiliating and frightening levels of racist abuse.

Muslim women wearing hijab remain the bellwether for attitudes towards their communities, with harassment against them peaking after major terrorist incidents as well as at times when Islam or immigration are in the news, such as during and immediately after the Brexit referendum campaign and the 2016 United States presidential election campaign that resulted in victory for Donald Trump. In 2012, after a protest in Sydney against the anti-Islamic film *Innocence of Muslims* ended in violent clashes between some of the protesters and the police, a hijab-wearing friend of mine in Canberra was confronted by a random stranger who offered to 'punch her for the police'. My smart, quick-witted friend had been taking martial arts classes, so I'm pretty sure that this bigot would have bitten off more than he could chew had he actually tried to land a punch on her. Luckily for him, Fatima told him that she'd prefer to be beaten up by the police rather than by him, and offered to call them on his behalf. He was left confused, but he can console himself that at least he didn't feel the force of Fatima's Anaconda Choke.

Stories like these generate a range of contradictory responses even within the same individual, never mind an entire community. My most immediate response was pure, undiluted outrage. What the hell makes anyone think that they can treat my friend and other women like her in such a manner? By what right does anyone assume a licence to stand in judgement on a total stranger and deliver the verdict in such a repulsive manner? Who does he think he is? Are we really supposed to respond to such abuse by showing how friendly and likeable and ordinary we can be?

And so the next impulse is to try to nurture, to make people see Fatima as the good-natured and funny and extraordinary-in-a-good-way person that she is, if you're willing to take a closer look. I'm tempted to explain her to others, to make them see her as I see her.

And then I'm back to outrage. Fatima is under no obligation to explain herself, and I ought not to take it upon myself to explain on her behalf.

Like terrorism, random incidents of abuse and harassment spread fear far beyond their immediate victims. Yet, despite such trepidation, the number of Muslim women wearing hijab increased steeply even as the stigma attached to it became ever more pronounced. Rhetorical calls to freedom such as 'why don't you wake up to yourself?' (a demand made of another young hijabi friend by an unknown woman on the street) do not invite a response other than bewilderment and, often much later, anger. The fact that many Muslim women living in the West articulately resisted their would-be 'saviours' generated aggressive attempts to awaken them from their supposed false consciousness. As part of the perceived Islamic infiltration of the West, they were no longer seen simply as helpless victims in need of rescue – they were also seen as a threat to be contained.

Women and girls who fall victim to racist assaults are generally portrayed as collateral damage in a conflict between men. The high rates of racist vilification and harassment of Muslim women are explained by their vulnerability and (in the case of those who wear hijab) their visibility. However, the 'visible soft target' explanation understates the extent to which Muslim women have come to be regarded as a dangerous and threatening element in their own right, not just as adjuncts to their men. Muslim women are increasingly perceived not just as bystanders or puppets but as active collaborators in male wrongdoing. In an increasing number of cases, they are regarded as autonomous transgressors who must bear full responsibility for their misdeeds.

The Muslim woman who refuses 'rescue' is considered to be an agent of Islamisation by default. This assumption is applied not only to the relatively small number of women who actively participate in Islamist organisations and movements, but also to those whose performance of their religious identity does not conform to the Western concept of gender emancipation. Their resistance to adopting the broadly accepted social norms of liberation in their own lives is assumed to represent a commitment to imposing their religious and social values on other women, both Muslim and non-Muslim.

Veils, Veils, Veils

The fixation on veiling in its various forms of course long pre-dates 2001, with the face-veil in particular long regarded by many Muslims and non-Muslims alike as an instrument of female transgression. Visiting Constantinople as the wife of the British ambassador to Turkey in 1828, Lady Mary Montagu delighted in the 'liberty' bestowed by the face-veil:

> 'Tis very easy to see that they have more Liberty than we have, no Woman of what rank so ever being permitted to go in the streets without 2 muslins, one that covers her face all but her Eyes and another that hides the whole dress of her head and hangs halfway down her back … 'tis impossible for the most jealous Husband to know his wife when he meets her, and no Man dare either touch or follow a Woman in the Street. This perpetual Masquerade gives them entire Liberty of following their Inclinations without danger of Discovery.

The Egyptian moderniser Qasim Amin (often described as 'the father of Egyptian feminism'), on the other hand, disapproved of the face-veil for the same reason that Montagu had extolled it – its potential use as an instrument of feminine deception. In his 1899 book *The Liberation of Women*, he lamented that a woman wearing a face-veil 'need not be concerned that anyone might identify her and report that so-and-so or the wife of so-and-so was doing such-and-such. She can accomplish whatever she desires under the protection of her veil.' The veil in the form of a headscarf, however, was 'one of the permanent cornerstones of morality'. Despite his overall admiration for Western gender norms, he did not believe that Egyptian women should go so far as to emulate European forms of dress, since the West had 'gone too far' in exposing women to public view.

The founder of the Egyptian Feminist Union, Huda Shaarawi, provided another landmark moment when she removed her face-veil after her return from a visit to Europe in 1923. Mohja Kahf, however, disputes the description of this gesture as an 'unveiling', seeing it instead as a redefinition of the veil. For Kahf, Shaarawi should be regarded as 'the first to model in the public eye the modernist dress which constitutes what is today largely known as the hijab in most Islamist circles'. Public unveiling ceremonies were staged by the French colonial authorities in Algeria and by the governments of Iran and Turkey to illustrate the transition from tradition to modernity. Unveiling of both the face and hair became more common-place among middle-class urban women in the first decades after independence across Egypt and other Muslim-majority societies, with the unveiled woman seen as a symbol of a modern, progressive society.

As Leila Ahmed relates in *A Quiet Revolution*, the appearance of the 'new hijab' in Egypt and elsewhere in the Middle East was generated by the ascent of Islamist movements during the 1970s and 1980s. The rising popularity of the hijab caused fear among those for whom it represented 'an augury of possibly unwelcome and even menacing changes to come'. However, as the new style of covering became a fashion trend among women with a diverse range of political perspectives across the Muslim world, it ceased to be a signifier of Islamism or even of a high degree of religiosity. Nor did it signify a retreat from public life – rather, it often communicated a woman's determination to advance her education and career in mixed-gender settings beyond the home. And women in many lower-class communities had never unveiled in the first place.

In Muslim communities in the West, too, the new hijab was initially adopted by women associated with Islamist networks before being taken up by a broad cross-section of Muslim women. And, rather than segregating its wearers from 'mainstream' society, its appeal lies in its capacity to allow them to blend into their educational and workplace surroundings, while still signalling their religious identity. Unlike *shalwar kameez* (a long tunic top over 'pyjama' pants worn by women from a range of religious communities in South Asia) and other regional outfits, the hijab can easily be teamed with contemporary fashion and with modified school, sports or service uniforms. Yet it continues to be represented as the insignia of an alien and unwanted identity.

In France, Muslim women and girls have been subjected to state regulation of their dress in the name of preserving French *laïcité*, or secularism, with the hijab a focus for controversy since the 1989 suspension of three girls who refused to remove their headscarves in school. Although the 2004 ban in that country on conspicuous religious symbols in public schools also prohibits large crosses, Jewish skullcaps and Sikh turbans, it is primarily directed at Muslim girls wearing headscarves. Historian Joan Wallach Scott argues in *The Politics of the Veil* that 'the other groups were included to undercut the charge of discrimination against Muslims and to comply with a requirement that such laws apply universally'. However, for migrants from the former French colonies, the state-imposed regulations also revived memories of the public unveiling ceremonies that had been staged under French colonial rule in Algeria – memories that remain uneasy despite the fact that the post-colonial governments of Algeria, Morocco and Tunisia have shown a similar hostility to the 'backward' practice of veiling.

The governments of some Muslim-majority societies (notably Turkey prior to 2013 and the former French colony of Tunisia until after the Arab Spring in 2011) have also imposed regulations against visibly religious dress in schools and government buildings. I was reminded of this fact by a conversation with a young headscarf-wearing Tunisian woman at the Grande Mosquée de Paris in 2008. I had expected her to tell me about the difficulties that she faced in wearing an item of clothing that had been so loudly reviled in France. Instead, she told me that she had come to study in Paris because her headscarf was prohibited on Tunisian university campuses (a ban that was lifted after the 2011 Arab Spring). Despite the anti-headscarf regulations in public schools, France was relatively liberal by comparison at that time. It was a useful reminder that there is no single trajectory to women's experiences and that these differing personal histories will inevitably shape their responses to their current circumstances.

Following the precedent established by France, similar prohibitions of hijab in public spaces such as courtrooms were introduced elsewhere in Europe and mooted by right-wing commentators and politicians in Britain, Australia, Canada and the United States. In those locations where the notion of regulation failed to gain support from the major political parties, the shadow of the 'hijab debates' contributed to an atmosphere in which holding women accountable for their form of dress was rationalised as a legitimate feminist exercise – even when undertaken by male authority figures not known for their feminist sympathies.

In response, Muslim spokeswomen and community representatives developed an articulate counter-narrative, describing hijab as a woman's personal choice. This emphasis on choice represented a shift away from a focus on modesty, which the first wave of hijabis had emphasised as a source of empowerment. Their headscarves signalled that they wished to be judged for their intellect and their personal values rather than for their physical attributes, which were for the private enjoyment of their husbands. Hijabis were said to be prioritising intellectual and spiritual development ahead of the expensive and time-consuming demands of elaborate hairstyles and revealing clothing. And, as Rafia Zakaria notes in her 2017 book *Veil*, the French ban also contributed to the claim that the hijab was a religious requirement for observant Muslim women since it 'forced a confrontation where an argument for not banning the headscarf relied for its strength on the false premise that it was an essential for Muslim practice'.

However, while modesty and religious obligation remain key rationales, Muslim women have responded to post-

9/11 hostility by emphasising the hijab's compatibility with Western lifestyles, not to mention the pleasures of global fashion. It signifies not separatism, but hybridity – a sentiment most overtly expressed by the women who have donned their national flags as headscarves in a gesture that may be read as celebration, defiance or both. The French women and girls who wore *tricolore* hijabs during the 2004 protests against the newly imposed prohibition on visibly religious symbols in state schools sent a clear statement about their entitlement to express both their religious and their national identity. The *Sun* newspaper's 2014 front-page image of a woman wearing a Union Jack hijab under the headline 'United Against IS', however, was seen as a gesture of exclusion rather than inclusion, with Nesrine Malik observing in the *Guardian* that, while many Muslims have condemned Islamic State of their own accord, 'to have it demanded of you is different. And to have it linked to your nationality via the Union Jack is a threat. It attached conditions to that nationality that others do not have to meet.' And, indeed, in 2016 the 'Making a Stand' campaign which was the topic of The *Sun*'s front-page splash was revealed to have been secretly funded by the British Home Office.

But perhaps the most famous flag-hijab was the stars and stripes worn by Bangladeshi American Munira Ahmed for a 2007 photograph that became the basis for a portrait by the artist Shepard Fairey which was printed out and carried by thousands of protestors during the massed marches in opposition to newly elected President Donald Trump. As Ahmed told the *Guardian* for a profile which described her as 'the woman who became the face of the Trump resistance', 'It's about saying that I'm as American as you are.'

In 2004, Lebanese-born Constable Maha Sukkar became the first police officer in Australia to wear hijab as part of her uniform, dismissing claims that her Velcro-fastened headscarf might interfere with her work. And Australian Muslim women became enthusiastic consumers of the growing international market for Islamic sportswear. And, as we have already seen, Lebanese-born Australian designer Aheda Zanetti designed and manufactured a high-quality local modest swimsuit under a catchy brand name – the burqini.

Yet the hijab retained its status as the symbol of an alien and threatening ideology, regardless of whether it was chosen by or imposed upon the woman concerned. In Australia, then Liberal MP Bronwyn Bishop rejected the suggestion that some Muslim women had 'chosen' to wear the hijab by saying that she could not accept 'someone who wants to be a little bit of a slave, or a little bit subservient. The fact of the matter is that in this country, freedom is defined by our law, and that's the standard, not someone else's definition of what they think freedom might be.'

Whether as victims or as rebels, hijabis came to be regarded as the standard-bearers of Muslim communities in the West, regardless of the fact that the majority of Muslim women in those communities wear headscarves only part-time, if at all.

Regardless of such alarmist attitudes, however, the heightened visibility of confident, articulate (not to mention stylish) hijabis gradually caused the headscarf to lose much of its political and media frisson. And, in his landmark 2009 'new beginning' speech in Cairo, US President Barack Obama sought to refocus the discourse on women's rights, saying, 'I reject the view of some in the West that a woman who chooses to cover her hair is somehow less equal, but I do believe that a woman who is denied an education is denied equality.' The next phase of the moral panic, then, centred on the burqa and its place (or otherwise) within Western societies.

In a speech to both houses of parliament in June 2009 at the Chateau of Versailles, then-French President Nicolas Sarkozy proclaimed:

> The problem of the burqa is not a religious problem, it's a problem of liberty and women's dignity. I want to say solemnly, the burqa is not welcome in France. In our country, we can't accept women prisoners behind a screen, cut off from all social life, deprived of all identity. That's not our idea of freedom.

Joan Wallach Scott described this speech as a reaction not only to internal events in France but also to Obama's Cairo speech, with its rebuttal of the claim that the hijab was a symbol of inferiority. Others were reminded of Fanon's observation about veiled women in the then-French colony of Algeria, 'This woman who sees without being seen frustrates the conqueror. There is no reciprocity. She does not yield herself, does not give herself, does not offer herself.'

I saw only a couple of women with their faces covered during a 2008 visit to Paris, despite the fact that my daughter and I had stayed with the family of a French Moroccan friend in a suburb with a significant north African population. And, as academic Nilufar Ahmed points out, the legislative documents in support of the 2011 legislation banning the face-veil stated that it was worn by only 1,900 women, or 0.04 per cent of the French Muslim population. Even this figure is thought to be a significant overestimate. Yet, despite its peripheral role in French life, Sarkozy's speech elevated the burqa to the top of the political agenda not just in France but across Europe and beyond. Burqas were denounced for disrupting the boundary between private and public space as legislation outlawing face-covering was introduced in France, Belgium, the Netherlands and Denmark. Sara R. Farris notes that 'feminist opposition to the anti-veil law, as well as alternative feminist stances concerning the mobilization of gender equality against Muslim citizens in France, has not been absent. On the contrary, it has been perhaps the most vigorous in Europe.' However, she notes that these voices of dissent have not been granted the same degree of public exposure as those of the femonationalists who supported the ban.

While calls for state-imposed regulation failed to gain political traction in the United Kingdom, North America and Australia, Muslim women were nonetheless subjected to a savage media and political onslaught. In Australia, journalist Virginia Haussegger, recently returned from a visit to Afghanistan, described her shock at seeing a 'hideously shrouded figure' in a Canberra shopping mall and called for Australia to implement a European-style ban. And police reports of an armed hold-up by a cross-dressing 'burqa bandit' who had held up a cash-distributor in Sydney's south prompted Liberal Senator Cory Bernardi to claim that the burqa 'is emerging as the preferred disguise of bandits and ne'er-do-wells'. More recently, in 2018 former British Foreign Secretary Boris Johnson created political waves during the fraught prelude to Britain's scheduled exit from the European Union by publishing an article in which he ridiculed Muslim women who veil their faces as looking like letter boxes or bank robbers.

Joumanah El Matrah from the Islamic Women's Welfare Council of Victoria (now the Australian Muslim Women's Centre for Human Rights), in commenting on these 'veil wars', has stated that:

> a significant amount of Muslim women's time 'on air' has been used to either explain the hijab or advocate women's right to wear it. There are many consequences of this but two urgent issues are that Muslim women increasingly appear incapable of addressing any other issue and that in restricting ourselves to this topic, an opportunity has been created for Muslim men to monopolise and define Islam.

Muslim women themselves hold far more ambivalent attitudes towards the niqab and/or the burqa than towards headscarves. Most of those who have grown up in Australia have had little or no contact with women who cover their faces. Some of those who cover their hair have supported moves to prohibit face-coverings. In 2010, Aziza Abdel-Halim, president of the Australian Women's National

Network, who herself wears hijab, told *The Age* with regard to Cory Bernardi's 'burqa bandit' remarks, 'If [the burqa] opens the way for criminal acts then, as Muslims, we have to think about it. I see nothing wrong with saying to women "Don't wear it in public". I see the senator's point. A lot of Muslim women would see his point.' However, others felt obligated to respond to racialised scaremongering by defending the entitlement of women to cover their faces if they so choose, even as they contest the claim that the practice is recommended in Islam.

This desire to show solidarity gained momentum as public discussion about face-veiling became louder and uglier. When Sydney glass-sculptor Sergio Redegalli painted a mural on the exterior wall of his studio in 2010 showing a burqa-wearing woman with a strike sign across her face beneath the slogan 'SAY NO TO BURQAS', Aziza Abdel-Halim, who only a few months earlier had said that she saw Cory Bernardi's point about the need to impose a ban on the burqa, was now reported by journalist Henry Budd as saying that Redegalli's mural was disrespectful and insulting and that wearing the burqa was a matter of 'personal choice'.

Once again, Muslim women were cast in the dual roles of victim and perpetrator. The consensus seemed to be that concealment of one's identity in public by an infinitesimally small number of Muslim women in Western societies can be described as bad manners at best and a potential weapon for criminals and terrorists at worst.

Tensions were even more fraught in September 2014 when Australia's national security alert was raised from medium to high and the government announced a new suite of anti-terrorism legislation to combat the threat from Islamic State. Cory Bernardi renewed his call for a burqa ban, this time with the support of then-Palmer United Senator Jacqui Lambie, who issued a statement proclaiming: 'Now we're at war with the sharia extremists and Australia has been placed on a heightened terrorism alert – we can't have anyone hiding their identity in public. It now becomes an important national security issue.' A few days later, an eighteen-year-old Muslim youth was shot dead by police after allegedly attempting to stab two officers outside a suburban Melbourne police station during a meeting to discuss the cancellation of his passport. Yet again, community groups reported a spike in the harassment and abuse of Muslim women.

I felt a sense of apprehension mingled with defiance, then, as I arranged my headscarf before travelling out to attend a conference at the Hume Islamic Youth Centre in Melbourne. The star guest at the conference was Yvonne Ridley, the British journalist who had risen to prominence when she was briefly detained by the Taliban in Afghanistan after 11 September 2001 – an experience that led her to convert to Islam. The *Daily Telegraph*'s report on the conference had described Ridley as a 'firebrand convert' who had allegedly defined suicide bombings as 'martyrdom operations'.

However, the conference and the youth centre that hosted it provided its attendees with a place of refuge from the political tensions outside. A woman who wore niqab told me that she had faced a heightened level of aggression since Jacqui Lambie's ban-the-burqa spiel the previous week. 'They yell at me while I'm driving. Men going [wolf-whistle] and screaming, "Rip it off!"' Another young woman in hijab said she was reluctant to leave her home suburb of Broadmeadows – 'Muslim central'. Outside the safety of her local neighbourhood, she'd had people chase her, yelling at her to go back to where she came from. Ridley entertained her female audience with her earthy northern English humour and her anecdotes about crossing the border into Afghanistan under the cover of her burqa ('like the invisibility cloak from *Harry Potter*') only to be arrested when her donkey bolted, revealing the camera she had hidden beneath the cloak.

Asked about Jacqui Lambie's burqa statement, Ridley said, 'I don't often criticise women, but she [Lambie] epitomises the term "daft bint". She's either incredibly ignorant or politically stupid, and I'm not sure which. What I would suggest to her is stop digging and apologise, pet, and do it quickly.' Ridley claimed that she had never yet met a niqabi who had been forced to wear the veil. 'And if there are men out there who force their wives to wear the niqab in public, then by banning it they've confined them to the house. If these women exist, then the niqab gave them the freedom to get out of the house.'

Attempts to regulate Muslim women's dress in Australia reached new heights of absurdity the following week with the announcement that visitors wearing facial coverings into Federal Parliament would be confined to a separate glassed-in gallery usually reserved for schoolchildren. This measure was introduced by then-Speaker Bronwyn Bishop, who was already deeply unpopular among Muslim women for her calls, a decade earlier, for the hijab to be banned in public schools. As many politicians and commentators pointed out, the ban was difficult to justify on security grounds given that all visitors to Parliament House have to pass through an airport-style security check and that there was no evidence that anyone wearing a face-covering had ever attempted to visit Parliament House anyway. The parliamentary burqa ban was withdrawn at the request of the prime minister before it was ever implemented, but the ill-feeling that it generated was much longer lasting – if for no other reason than the monumental amount of time and energy that this fracas had consumed.

The parliamentary burqa ban was still in effect when I left Australia to visit Pakistan, where face-veils of course are a far more commonplace sight and where women dressed in that manner have become members of Parliament. 'But this is discrimination!' Samia Raheel Qazi said when I told her about Australia's 'burqas in Parliament' fracas. 'You are allowing a woman with bikini, with nude in your Parliament but you are not allowing a woman with a covered face to sit in a Parliament. So I think this is discrimination, and I protest on it.'

Raheel Qazi had her own experience of parliamentary face-veiling. When she was appointed a member of Pakistan's National Assembly under newly introduced gender quotas, she was told that she would need to be photographed with an uncovered face for her parliamentary ID card. She described her response:

But they allow us [to keep our face-veils] because I protest on it. It is my religious obligation, yes? I don't agree that if you don't cover your face, you are not a good Muslim. It is not good and bad Muslim – it is my choice. I belong to a religious and political party whose workers believe that their leader should be with a covered face. But at the same time, my daughter is not covering her face. We both have choices – to cover or to cover not.

However, Qazi's commitment to the principle of choice relates to the face-veil rather than to the headscarf, which she and her party strenuously promote as an essential element of faith.

Reading Facial Demeanour

Even in societies such as those of Australia, Britain, Canada and the United States that have not attempted to outlaw the face-veil, it is regularly described as a breach of social etiquette which denies others the opportunity to read one's facial expression. In 2006, some years before the face-veil bans in France, Jack Straw MP, member of the Labour Party and Leader of the House of Commons, wrote a widely publicised column for his local newspaper in which he stated that, while he would never force anyone to remove their veil, he did request that women meeting with him uncover their faces. After all, Straw argued, the value of a meeting as opposed to a phone call is that 'you can see what the other person means, not just hear what they say'.

As Sara R. Farris relates, the French philosopher Élisabeth Badinter provided a more elaborate valorisation of the importance of 'the face':

> In this possibility of being looked at without being seen, and to look at the other without him/her being able to see you, I see the satisfaction of a triple perverse enjoyment: the enjoyment of one's supremacy over another, the enjoyment of the exhibitionist, and the enjoyment of the voyeur.

These were, she concludes, 'very sick women'.

In 2011, the government of Stephen Harper in Canada introduced a rule directing women to remove the face-veils when taking the oath of citizenship on the grounds that it was 'anti-woman' and that, unless a woman's face was uncovered, it would not be possible to know whether or not she had actually recited the oath. Like Straw, Harper regarded an uncovered face as essential to polite behaviour. 'It's offensive that someone would try to hide their identity at the very moment where they are committing to join the Canadian family.' Eventually overturned by the Supreme Court in 2015, the regulation had nonetheless fulfilled its function of marking Muslim women as unworthy and ill-mannered family members.

However, veils are not the only means of refraining from facial communication. I recall a conversation with a recently arrived Hindu migrant from India who described Australians as having 'closed faces'. We allow our own facial expressions to serve as burqas, deterring others from making eye contact, let alone unnecessary small talk. And this is increasingly augmented by the use of smart phones and headphones, which allow their users to traverse public space insulated by technology from fellow-commuters, passers-by or over-lengthy conversations with service personnel.

The belief in the value of facial expression in communication – so-called 'demeanour evidence' – has been debated in various legal cases over whether women may be forced to remove their face-veils when giving evidence in court. Judicial rulings on niqabs in courtrooms in the UK, Australia, Canada and the United States have ranged from ordering the woman to remove her veil, to allowing her to give evidence via closed-circuit TV or in a closed courtroom in the presence of only those men who were essential to the proceedings of the case.

These cases are generally seen as placing the right to freedom of religion against the need for lawyers and jurors to be able to assess facial expressions as well as verbal evidence during cross-examination. Perhaps the most troubling such example was a criminal case in Canada in which a woman who had alleged a long history of childhood sexual abuse was told that she would need to remove her niqab if she wished to testify against her alleged abuser. She declined to do so and the charges were dropped. As the dissenting judge noted, the ruling 'essentially means that sexual abuse complainants, whose evidence will invariably be contested, will be forced to choose between laying a complaint and wearing a niqab, which may be no meaningful choice at all'.

The high value placed on demeanour evidence has been questioned by academic researchers and commentators who point out its susceptibility to bias and false interpretations. But the rationale for ordering women to uncover in parliament, in a courthouse or school or on the street does not have to make sense. Its logic lies in establishing the entitlement of the dominant culture to order her to do so and to open her to its gaze. As Sherene H. Razack observes, 'Unavailable, she is simultaneously feared and desired.'

Fear of and Desire for the Female Muslim Consumer

Generation M: Young Muslims Changing the World, by Shelina Janmohamed, focuses on the role of Muslims (including Muslim women) as consumers rather than as victims or as suspects. As the vice-president of Ogilvy Noor, 'the world's first bespoke global Islamic branding practice for building brands with Muslim audiences', she sees rising prosperity among Muslim consumers around the world as an incentive for companies and societies to promote themselves in ways that are attractive to this lucrative market. 'Societies and corporations which fail to embrace Gen M will miss out on the prosperity that they generate. They do not hesitate to exercise their power as consumers.'

Middle-class professional Muslims living in the West are cited as 'good Muslims' in the good Muslim/bad Muslim binary, in large part because of their appeal as consumers. Halal-certified groceries, sharia-compliant financial services, beauty products and of course modest

113

fashion are cited as products that can enhance access to this promising emerging market. As Kashmira Gander observed in an October 2017 article for the *Independent* on the mainstream success of modest clothing, 'it would be naïve to ignore that modest clothing is another way to market towards consumers from Muslim-majority countries with young populations and many, many petro-dollars'. The loss of sales to the valuable Muslim consumer market is regularly cited as one of the 'costs' of Islamophobia, with reports that the French ban on burqas has led to an exodus of wealthy Arab customers from Paris to London.

However, the celebration of the soft power of the Muslim middle class both excludes lower-class Muslims and plays into Islamophobic representations of Muslim consumer power as a threat that is forcing Muslims and non-Muslims alike to conform to Islamic norms or be excluded from their own society. For those entrenched in anti-Muslim racism, the soft power of consumerism and branding is as threatening as the hard power of armies and terrorist attacks. Anger at this alleged corporate sell-out to Islamisation is manifested in tabloid and social media outrage when supermarkets wish their customers 'happy Ramadan', feature visibly Muslim women in their advertising, or introduce products that are seen as catering for Muslim customer preferences. When Marks & Spencer announced that full-body swimsuits would be available for sale in its UK stores in March 2016 (a few months before the Nice attack and subsequent burqini bans), the French minister for women's rights Laurence Rossignol responded by saying that 'You cannot pass off as trivial and harmless the fact that big brands are investing in a market that puts Muslim women in a situation of having to wear that', before describing women who supported the modest clothing market as like 'negroes who supported slavery'. As reported by *Harper's Bazaar*, Pierre Bergé, the former partner of fashion icon Yves Saint Laurent, was similarly aghast, proclaiming that 'Creators should have nothing to do with Islamic fashion. Designers are there to make women more beautiful, to give them their freedom, not to collaborate with this dictatorship which imposes this abominable thing by which we hide women and make them live a hidden life.' However, this fulminating failed to convince Marks & Spencer to retreat from what is proving a successful marketing strategy for a range of mainstream labels. Brands ranging from Dolce & Gabbana to Nike to H&M have all introduced modest fashion lines in recent years, and, as noted by author of *Brand Islam* Faegheh Shirazi, the market for modest swimwear has been saturated by more affordable imports from China.

Both fear of and desire for the Muslim female consumer were on show in the coverage of the *Faith, Fusion, Fashion* exhibition's tour of South East Asia. DFAT's announcement of the launch of the exhibition in Malaysia cited the event's contribution to 'the obvious economic benefits' of the event, given that the modest fashion market was forecast to reach US$368 billion by 2025. This economic rationale drew support from some figures on the right, with the newsletter of the libertarian Centre for Independent Studies think tank publishing an article by Peter Kurti which stated:

When an Aussie fashion designer shows Muslim women how they can be both contemporary *and* modest, we should embrace it as part of our open multicultural society – and promote it. After all, the DFAT exhibition was destined for Kuala Lumpur and not Klosters. Muslim women in Malaysia are going to buy their clothes from somewhere: why not encourage it to be from Australia?

'Fashion diplomacy', after all, makes sound economic sense.

But, regardless of their attire, Muslim women undertake this type of diplomacy in their everyday lives as they patiently (or sometimes not so patiently) navigate the minefield of prejudice and discrimination. It is difficult to suppress the reflex to respond to exclusion and marginalisation by listing the economic and diplomatic 'benefits' that Muslim women bring to their communities and societies. But this level of self-justification is not required from 'mainstream' members of society. Why, then, should it be expected of Muslim women?

While some non-Muslim consumers may be deterred by signifiers such as halal certification and visibly Muslim women in advertising, for others Generation M signifies a cosmopolitan and desirable lifestyle brand. A glamorous young Gen M hijab-wearing photographer was a prominent feature of the short-lived Pepsi Max advertisement featuring Kendall Jenner resolving an unspecified conflict by handing a police officer a Pepsi at a Black Lives Matter-style protest. Pepsi withdrew the advertisement and apologised after a snowstorm of criticism for its attempt to co-opt the power of anti-racism, but the incident had illustrated the value placed on its target market.

Dee Madigan, advertising director and regular panellist on *The Gruen Transfer* (a popular Australian television panel show which focuses on the advertising industry), harnessed her own brand and that of her industry to the anti-racist cause in response to what was referred to as 'the billboards incident' in January 2017. The billboard in question, featuring two primary school-aged girls wearing hijabs and waving Australian flags, had been commissioned by the Victorian state government to promote its Australia Day celebrations. It was removed from its site in the Melbourne suburb of Cranbourne after the media company which owns the space received a deluge of threatening and abusive messages initiated by the far-right Patriots United Front, which described the billboard as 'making every effort to redefine your nation and gradually erase you from history'. In response, Madigan initiated a crowdfunding campaign to re-erect the billboard under the hashtag #PutThemBackUp. Prominent Muslim community leaders and politicians from both sides of parliament endorsed the campaign, which quickly gathered pace, raising more than $120,000 in less than twenty-four hours.

However, Australia's national day marks the anniversary of white settlement and the dispossession of the Aboriginal and Torres Strait Islander people, with 'Invasion Day' a focus for protests as well as celebration. Given these sensitivities, a cohort of mostly second- and third-generation Muslims quickly moved to disassociate themselves from the campaign to reinstate the billboards whose purpose was to promote Australia's contentious national day. Comedian and anti-racism activist Aamer Rahman posted a comment on Twitter in which he stated: 'Raising over $100k to state your support for Muslims to take part in genocide celebrations is ridiculous. This type of lame, assimilationist sentimentality is useless. Truly a novel and expensive way of throwing Aboriginal people under the bus.' Other Muslim writers expanded on these criticisms. In an article for the National Indigenous Television (NITV) website, Aboriginal, Chinese-Malaysian and Muslim writer Eugenia Flynn observed that 'We know that an imagine of two young girls, smiling with the Australian flag, is not meant to cause intentional offence, but symbolises the indoctrination of new migrants into the national project.' When the new billboards were unveiled, the words '26th January' had been removed, with the logo simply stating, 'Happy Australia Day' (the word 'happy' not having featured on the original billboards). As Eugenia Flynn wrote, 'To say that the new billboards are more offensive that the original is an understatement.'

The #PutThemBackUp campaign, then, provided a means for white Australians to reassure themselves that (as Dee Madigan had proclaimed) the racists did not represent them, as well as for the advertising and public relations industries to broadcast their ethical potential. As the industry publication *AdNews* proclaimed, Madigan had raised enough money to 'put up 17 billboards, 500 street posters and seven full-page newspaper ads – all the while taking on Twitter trolls and ultimately showing the power of the ad industry'. Madigan herself was quoted as saying,

'We [the advertising industry] don't always have to be the bad guys ... the success of this campaign shows that we can be part of the solution.'

Rescue missions from white racism, then, can be as problematic in their way as are rescue missions from Islamic patriarchy, based as they are on the shared assumption that Muslim women are incapable of rescuing themselves. And the celebration of a particular type of Muslim female consumer (generally presented as middle class, fluent in English, tertiary educated and attractive according to conventional Western beauty norms) risks further marginalising those women who do not conform to this standard.

Conclusion

How, then, are Muslim women to respond to these twinned representations of victim and aggressor? After all, it is not our collective responsibility to act as therapists in the treatment of other people's paranoia and moral panic. Yet many of us feel compelled to respond, whether by soothing the fearful, standing up to the bullies or, all too often, both. And so we find ourselves in a catch-22 situation. We've responded to representations of victimhood by highlighting success stories – Muslim women who are not subserviently remaining within the patriarchal boundaries of the home, but who are attaining educational, professional and social achievements. In the course of the past decade, Australian Muslim women have moved from a position of inaudibility (note I do not use the word 'invisibility' because the media's obsession with the hijab ensured their visibility) to a situation in which a diverse range of Muslim women are regular contributors to Australian public discussions. Visibly Muslim women have made frequent appearances as the 'voice of reason' during heated panel discussions and public debates. In Australia, Susan Carland, Sameh Habib and Randa Abdel-Fattah have participated in media forums such as ABC's *Q&A* and SBS's *Insight*, contributed opinion pieces to major newspapers and received public recognition for their work. Susan Carland was included on the Fairfax media website's list of the twenty most influential female voices of 2012. Profiles of path-breaking Muslim women in activities that are perceived as outside the norms of their religious community have become a regular media feature, including positive stories about women such as Maha Sukkar, the first Australian police officer to be allowed to incorporate her hijab as part of her uniform, Miriam Silva, 'an outspoken female senior manager who wears hijab in her role heading commercial operations at one of the country's oldest and most conservative rural companies', and Royal Australian Navy Captain Mona Shindy, who, like Sukkar, wears hijab as part of her uniform. In the United Kingdom, Nadiya Jamir Hussain became a household name as the 2015 winner of *The Great British Bake Off*. In the United States, journalist Noor Tagouri made headlines around the world in 2016 when she became the first hijab-wearing woman to appear in *Playboy* magazine. Featured in the magazine's 'Renegades' issue as one of 'eight men and women who aren't afraid to break the rules', Tagouri was photographed in front of a bullet-ridden stars and stripes, wearing her headscarf with a leather jacket, T-shirt, jeans and an appropriately renegade scowl. The magazine described her as 'a badass activist' who is 'making a surprisingly bold case for modesty'. Indeed, the regular focus on female Muslim success stories has reached the point where the Muslim-woman-breaking-stereotypes story has become a stereotype in itself. Up-and-coming women joke about not wanting to be dragged into performing the stereotype of the Muslim woman as stereotype-breaker.

According to the ever-shriller voices of anti-Muslim scaremongering, stories such as these simply confirm the successful infiltration of Islam into Western society. Muslim women who carry their religious identity into public space – most obviously in the form of their dress but also in other practices such as prayer, creating a market for halal food, or even abstinence from alcohol consumption at workplace social functions – have embedded alien social norms into 'mainstream' society. Muslim women in the West are urged to breach the confines of their domestic space in order to repudiate the perceived patriarchal boundaries of their religious identity, but they are expected to leave the visible markers of their religion behind them when they venture into the public realm. Muslim women are allowed into this space on the condition that they not only follow the law of the land, but also that they accept the capacity and entitlement of its dominant forces to reprove them for perceived breaches of etiquette.

4

PROXY WARS

*Because these Western feminists manifest an almost
neurotic fear of offending a minority group's culture, the
situation of Muslim women creates a huge philosophical
problem for them.*

— Ayaan Hirsi Ali, *Nomad*, 2014

Proxy wars – conflicts between nations in which neither of
the major combatants directly engages the other – provide
a means to wage battle without risking the mutual annihi-
lation that might ensue in a direct conflict between the
main players. The Cold War was dominated by a series of
proxy conflicts between the superpowers in locations
ranging from Korea to Vietnam to El Salvador to – of
course – Afghanistan.

Proxy wars insulate the major combatants from the
devastation of the battlefield, but exact a far higher price

from the proxies themselves. Such wars continue to be fought in the post-9/11 era, with Syria, Iraq, Yemen and Lebanon providing staging grounds for conflicts between outside actors such as the United States, Iran, Turkey, Saudi Arabia, Israel and Russia. And, thanks to 'the Muslim issue', as it has come to be known, even culture wars over competing political and social values within the West can now be fought by proxy.

In the aftermath of 11 September 2001, political thinking in North America, Britain and Australia under-went a process of apparent ideological consolidation as politicians and commentators set out to define just what it was that 'we' were defending in the War on Terror. This process was dominated by a sense that, during the decade prior to the 2001 attacks on New York and Washington, public discourse throughout the Anglosphere had lost the ideological certainties of the Cold War. Faced with an external enemy, it was now time to reassert our identity around everything that made 'us' different to (and better than) 'them'. Just as Afghanistan had provided the site for a proxy war between the United States and the Soviet Union, Muslims living in the West became the proxies in cultural civil wars within 'mainstream' society over issues ranging from free speech to multiculturalism to state funding for private education – and, perhaps most promi-nently of all, feminism and gender norms.

Evelyn Baring (later Lord Cromer), the British consul-general in Egypt for nearly a quarter of a century, famously provided the template for the appropriation of feminism by conservative men, denouncing Islam's degradation of women while serving as president of the Society Opposed to Women's Suffrage. Post-9/11 leaders such as George W. Bush and former Australia prime ministers John Howard and Tony Abbott have followed Cromer's lead in espousing the language of women's rights in order to justify attacks on Muslim societies and communities while enforcing socially conservative values on issues such as reproductive rights at home. This type of hypocrisy and political opportunism has damaged the feminist brand throughout the regions and communities colonised in its name. Commentators have claimed that the War on Terror serves as a reminder that, while feminism is no longer necessary in the post-feminist West, there are still women elsewhere who urgently need it. Sadly, however, feminists themselves have supposedly failed to fulfil the obligations of their own ideology.

Fearmongering around Muslims and gender has become increasingly securitised in the years since 9/11. As Arun Kundnani writes in his 2014 book *The Muslims are Coming*, while the early stages of the War on Terror had focused on the enemy as an organisational threat in the form of al-Qaeda to be fought primarily 'over there' in Afghanistan and Iraq, by the time of the Arab Spring in 2011 'the enemy had come to be understood as more than a single individual or organization; it was a set of ideas – radical Islam – that was defined vaguely enough that even the death of bin Laden would not halt the hundreds of billions of dollars the war involved.' In this new phase of the War on Terror, then, it is possible to give aid and comfort to the enemy by sharing a similar ideological terrain with them, even without providing material support to those undertaking or planning to undertake violent attacks. And conservative gender norms when held by Muslims, as opposed to other ethno-religious communities, are regarded as a troubling signifier of extremism. Internal differences of opinion on this topic among non-Muslims living in the West, however heated, are concealed beneath a veneer of faux consensus in order to locate Muslims (or at least 'bad Muslims') as the enemy within.

Within Muslim communities and societies, on the other hand, feminism is often characterised (or caricatured) as an alien and hostile force. In the fraught post 9/11 political atmosphere, Muslim women campaigning for women's rights are frequently accused of acting as proxies of the West; of using women's rights in order to introduce 'Western' sexual norms (in the form of sexual promiscuity and family breakdown) and to facilitate Western political hegemony. As Asma Barlas, author of *Believing Women in Islam*, observed in her Spinoza lecture in 2008:

> Muslim women are thus trapped between a large mainstream of conservatives and a small fringe of secularists and feminists who attack us for trying to un-read patriarchy from the Qur'an. (I have not even mentioned those non-Muslims who are invested in illiberal readings of the Qur'an or who want Muslims to scrap it.)

As one of the proxies in this culture war, I often had the surreal sense that I was simultaneously at the centre and on the sidelines of the battlefield of 'the Muslim issue'. Having published articles about Muslim-related topics, I was regularly contacted by figures from one or other (or both) sides of these battles – experiences that left me with the sense that 'the Muslim issue' in contemporary public life is used as a vehicle for other disputes and is seldom very much to do with Muslims at all.

'Where are the Western feminists?'

For commentators who like their feminist-bashing mixed with a good shot of Islamophobia, it has become a popular pastime to accuse 'Western feminists' of abandoning their Muslim sisters to the brutality of Muslim men. Western feminists are accused of being dilettantes, so caught up in their own petty battles over issues such as body image and pole dancing that they have chosen to ignore the life-and-death issues facing their sisters in Saudi Arabia, Somalia and Afghanistan. Worse still, feminists and left-wing multiculturalists have acted as fellow-travellers for Islamist forces within their own society, prioritising multiculturalism over gender equity when faced by misogyny in migrant communities. Not only does this leave Muslim women and girls within those communities at the mercy of their menfolk, it also places at risk the very values – free speech, religious tolerance, secularism – that have allowed feminism to flourish in Western societies. Australian authors Zora Simic and Monica Dux describe this as an attack on 'straw feminism'. 'The straw feminist is an apologist for Islam, so obsessed with anti-racism and multiculturalism that she is unable to save her Muslim sisters.'

The oppression of Muslim women has become a rhetorical device to silence non-Muslim women who dare to complain about their lot, with feminists routinely told to prioritise the battle against Muslim cultural practices such as forced marriage, honour killings and, in particular, female genital mutilation ahead of their own self-indulgent concerns. Prominent evolutionary biologist and atheist Richard Dawkins took up this cudgel to attack young feminist atheist blogger Rebecca Watkins after she posted a short video in which she complained about an unwanted sexual advance that she had received in the elevator of her hotel during an atheist conference. During the subsequent 'elevatorgate' fracas, Dawkins posted a long comment to Watkins' blog. Opening with 'Dear Muslima', the letter satirises an American feminist's supposed indifference to the pleas of her persecuted Muslim 'sister':

> Stop whining, will you. Yes, I know you had your genitals mutilated with a razor blade, and . . . yawn . . . don't tell me again, I know you aren't allowed to drive a car, and you can't leave the house without a male relative, and your husband is allowed to beat you, and you'll be stoned to death if you commit adultery. But stop whining, will you. Think of the suffering your poor American sisters have to put up with.

For commentators such as Dawkins, the alleged feminist 'failure' to rescue Muslim women is a blunt instrument with which to bludgeon the entire feminist enterprise. Graphic descriptions of female genital mutilation are often used in confrontations of this type in which the intention is not to raise awareness about the practice or support the women affected by it, but simply to undermine a woman or women over an unrelated issue. At times, such confrontations serve as a form of sexual harassment. This is most manifest in the graphic photographs of horrifically injured girls' genitals that have been emailed to myself and to other Muslim women. Given the supposed or actual age of the girls featured in such photographs, these images should be classified as child pornography. The banners at Reclaim Australia rallies proclaiming 'You keep your burqa, I'll keep my clitoris' are less disturbing, but serve a similarly confrontational purpose. Demands for the denunciation of female genital mutilation serve as a licence to strip Muslim women of what is assumed to be our prudish reluctance to discuss sexuality and intimate body parts. It's the verbal equivalent of tearing off a woman's headscarf.

For a hard-core of right-wing commentators, feminism's alleged reluctance to confront Islam is part of a broader left-wing sympathy for Islamism, consistent with the Left's long-standing affinity with totalitarian ideologies. For others, however, feminism should be celebrated as an achievement of Western civilisation which must be protected from those who would undermine its key tenets.

Is Multiculturalism (and Islam) Bad for Women?

Many of the issues that have dominated recent discussions of feminism and Muslim women were prefigured by Susan

Moller Okin in her 1999 essay 'Is Multiculturalism Bad for Women?' and the critical responses that it generated. According to Okin, while patriarchy continues to exist in all cultures and communities, liberal democracies have made more progress in addressing the inequities it produces than have many of the migrant communities that have settled in the West. Rather than encouraging these migrants to assimilate to the higher standard of behaviour prevalent in their new surroundings, multiculturalism prioritises group rights over individual rights at the expense of women and girls. The question therefore facing feminists in multi-cultural societies is 'What should be done when the claims of minority cultures or religions clash with the norm of gender equality that is at least formally endorsed by liberal states (however much they continue to violate it in practice)?' Feminists such as Leti Volpp and Uma Narayan took issue with Okin's binary and static view of Western liberal culture versus minoritised ethnic Others, pointing out the contested and hybrid nature of culture.

The War on Terror gave new impetus to these intra-feminist debates, as feminists took sides for or against the mission to rescue and/or discipline Muslim women. As Sara R. Farris relates, French feminists such as sociologist Christine Delphy and philosopher Elsa Dorlin denounced the appropriation of feminism by those attempting to discipline Muslim women via the antiveiling regulations. On the other side of the debate, US writer and psychotherapist Phyllis Chesler claimed that 'a postmodern and postcolonial feminism that passionately condemns Christianity and Judaism as the greatest danger to women's rights but dares not critique religiously supremacist Islam for this same reason' is responsible for 'the death of feminism', as she described it in her 2006 book of that title.

Somali-born writer and former Dutch politician Ayaan Hirsi Ali has become an important figurehead in these obituaries to feminism, reiterating the superiority of Western gender norms over those of 'lesser' civilisations – Islam in particular – and upbraiding Western feminists for failing to uphold their own values. In her 2016 video lecture for the conservative non-profit organisation PragerU on 'Why don't feminists fight for Muslim women?', she warned that:

> The current situation in Europe is deeply troubling: not only are Muslim women within Europe subject to considerable oppression in many ways, such norms now risk spreading to non-Muslim women who face harassment from Muslim men. One would think that Western feminists in the United States and Europe would be very disturbed by this obvious misogyny. But sadly, with few exceptions, this does not appear to be the case.

For Hirsi Ali, 'Western feminists and female Western leaders have a simple choice to make: either excuse the inexcusable or demand reform in cultures and religious doctrines that continue to oppress women.' The archetype of the 'good Muslim' spokeswoman in this discourse is Ayaan Hirsi Ali herself, who, as an enlightened 'native informant' and atheist, has advocated such disciplinary measures as compulsory gynaecological examinations of all girls from Muslim families in order to combat female genital mutilation (FGM) and admission tests for asylum-seekers to ensure that they will embrace the values of their new society.

Hirsi Ali's call for widely disparate elements within the West to present a united front against Islam is mirrored by her supporters' representation of Hirsi Ali herself as a figurehead that transcends national boundaries to represent the West as a whole. This rationale underpinned a campaign led by Bernard-Henri Lévy to grant French citizenship to Hirsi Ali after the Netherlands withdrew her security funding because of her US residency. In a 2006 essay, Lévy described Pakistan and Hirsi Ali as the two front lines in the 'War on Terror' – Pakistan as the headquarters of al-Qaeda and Hirsi Ali as 'personally, a sort of frontline because she is always in danger of losing her life for defending the ideas of liberal civilisation'.

However, concepts of gender norms and identity are far more fragmented within 'liberal civilisation' than is acknowledged by those claiming to be its front-line guardians.

Gender Segregation and Gender Identity

Gender-segregated student events on university campuses have triggered a series of moral panics in Australia, Canada and the United Kingdom. In the United Kingdom, there was a series of incidents in which various Islamic societies at different universities hosted lectures with separate seating areas for men and women. In response, the peak body representing the sector, Universities UK, issued guidance in November 2013 indicating that universities were legally obliged to respect a request from an external speaker for gender-segregated seating. This guidance was eventually withdrawn after a political and media furore, but the topic remained on the political agenda. In 2016, Britain's then-Prime Minister David Cameron singled out gender segregation in public buildings as one of the issues that his government would address in order to prevent British Muslims from becoming radicalised – a concern later echoed by his successor Theresa May.

A similar fracas broke out in Australia in 2013 after *The Australian* reported that signs at a public lecture held at the University of Melbourne (where I was based at the time) by the Muslim organisation Hikmah Way had directed 'sisters' to the back of the theatre and 'brothers' to the front. Reporter Rachel Baxendale added that 'gender segregation was also encouraged' at an on-campus information session for prospective volunteers at a forthcoming Islamic peace conference.

This event saw yet another alignment between a conservative male politician and a left-wing feminist. 'I just think it's un-Australian what's happened here and I can't understand for a second why Melbourne University would tolerate it,' proclaimed then-opposition leader Tony Abbott. Internationally renowned University of Melbourne gender studies professor Sheila Jeffreys, author of the book *Man's Dominion: The Rise of Religion and the Eclipse of Women's Rights*, was equally incensed, describing the meeting as 'a Rosa Parks moment'.

At first glance, Jeffreys' analogy – women (or blacks) to the back of the theatre (or bus), men to the front – seems uncontentious. However, this overlooks the distinction between public transport as an essential service and an event arranged by a student group as a voluntary social activity, organised to suit the preferences of the participants. And, spatially, photographs of the event illustrate that, as is usual in such venues, those seated at the back of the theatre looked down upon those in the front row. This reflects the most common arrangements in mosques, in which women's prayer space is often located on a balcony above the main prayer space. Even when, as is so often the case, this arrangement is intended to signify women's subordinate position, it is also provides them with a view of the male area while remaining out of sight themselves. Women do not necessarily experience back-row seats as disempowering. After all, it can provide them with the opportunity 'to see without being seen'. And, as Fanon noted – and as the panic over burqas illustrates – this invisibility is widely regarded as a dangerously subversive power that allows women to escape male surveillance and authority.

The panic over gender-segregated Muslim student events elides the plethora of single-sex spaces throughout British and Australian society, including schools and university campuses. David Cameron was criticised by his education secretary Michael Gove for having appointed a 'ridiculous' number of his fellow Eton Old Boys to his inner cabinet. As a devout Catholic who in his youth toyed with the idea of entering the priesthood, Tony Abbott is presumably very familiar with both gender-segregated spaces and gender hierarchy. And a quick search of the University of Melbourne's website at the time when it was under fire for allowing a gender-segregated Muslim event to take place on its premises reveals other 'gender-segregated' events by non-Muslim organisations, including a women-only morning tea and a women's self-defence class. 'Enjoy a relaxing morning tea, coffee and cake slice while you meet and mingle with your fellow female grad students' admittedly sounds a lot less contentious than Hikmah Way's lecture on 'Islamic Jihad in Syria and why great scholars' silence' [sic] – but that is a different issue.

I attended the Islamic Peace Conference in Melbourne that had made the headlines with its gender-segregated volunteers meeting. As usual at Islamic events, men were directed to pray in front of women during the outdoor prayers on the oval and, as is also commonplace, all the worshippers were given confusing instructions over a badly functioning sound system regarding which direction to turn in order to face Mecca.

However, once the attendees moved to the marquees for lectures, the MC directed 'men to my right, women to my left' and families with young children to a separate marquee where they would cause less disruption. As usual at Muslim events, the pleas to relocate the children were almost universally ignored and they remained with their mothers, grandmothers and aunts in the women's section of the main marquee.

The young women volunteers, in their conservative hijabs and high-visibility official vests, were keen to be of service to those having difficulty navigating the boggy, uneven ground and complicated arrangements at the conference. They showed every sign of taking pride in their role and the status it bestowed on them. They thrived rather than wilted in the gender-segregated space of the conference. This has been the dynamic at other gender-segregated events that I have attended in locations ranging from South East Asia to the Middle East, often hosted by very socially conservative movements. The Egyptian scholar Leila Ahmed writes that while gender segregation has denied Muslim women many opportunities, it has also given them the space to develop their own religious understanding 'which pays little or no attention to the utterances and exhortations of sheikhs or any sort of official figures'. Women will continue to seek those informal spaces where 'women's Islam' dominates – and religiously conservative men would not like a lot of what gets said there.

All the same, gender segregation is a hotly debated issue among Muslims themselves – not only in the context of its most acute manifestations such as in Taliban-governed Afghanistan or contemporary Saudi Arabia, but also with regard to Muslim communities in the West. African American Muslim scholar Amina Wadud made international headlines when she led mixed-gender prayers in New York in 2005, contrary to the dominant belief that, while women could take the role of imam in leading prayers for other women, only men could lead prayers for male or mixed-gender congregations.

Wadud's book *Inside the Gender Jihad* won her an ardent fan club among Muslim feminists all over the world. When

I met her in Canberra on her first visit to Australia, my mobile beeped every few seconds with envious text messages from young Muslim women around Australia. Guests at a dinner held in her honour nervously asked whether she planned to lead mixed-gender prayers during her visit to Australia. She replied that, while she was open to invitations to do so, it was not a gesture that she felt compelled to repeat at regular intervals.

Muslim women in the West have mostly focused their campaigns not on desegregating Muslim religious space, but on providing Muslim women with equal space to men. The women's sections in some of the great mosques of the world are located on upper-level balconies that provide a spectacular view of latticework screens, chandeliers and frescos the details of which are too far removed for those at ground level to appreciate. However, the women's sections at most mosques in the West are far less salubrious – where they even exist. Muslim community leaders justify the unequal amount of space allocated to men and women in mosques on the grounds that far fewer women than men attend Friday prayers, which most Islamic scholarship regards as compulsory for men but optional for women in order to allow them to fulfil their responsibilities at home. Some mosques have chosen to regard this dispensation as a prohibition, while others have chosen to restrict the women's space to overcrowded, airless rooms. The late Jamila Hussain, a law lecturer at the University of Sydney, undertook a survey which found that, in many Australian mosques, women are not just allocated separate prayer space from men but also separate, and often inadequate, space for performing the obligatory ablutions (meanwhile the men wash at a picturesque fountain in a sunny court-yard). In some mosques, women must descend a flight of stairs to a basement to wash before climbing yet more stairs to an upper-level balcony to pray. For women with impaired mobility (including me), that's an impossible challenge, particularly given that, even if we manage to access the women's space, we may not be able to see or hear the imam as he delivers the sermon.

Even campaigns for what could reasonably be described as moderate reforms have met with significant pushback from some male Muslim community leaders. Keysar Trad, leader of the Islamic Friendship Association of Australia, responded to media coverage of Jamila Hussain's report on the need for improved female space in mosques by conflating the issue of equal space with gender-integrated space. He noted in an article for *Crikey* that the prostrations involved in Muslim prayer often bring a worshipper's face into close proximity of the backside of the person praying in front of him. Hussain's campaign, then, represented an assault on the privacy of Muslim women and risked attracting the wrong kind of convert – men who signed up in the hope of becoming physically close to Muslim women during prayer.

The 'Open My Mosque' social media campaign established in 2015 by activist Anita Nayyar has highlighted similar problems with regard to female access to mosques in Britain. As journalist Remona Aly reports, 28 per cent of British mosques provide no access to women, while in many others the designated women's space is 'often

137

cramped [and] fails health and safety standards'. However, Aly also notes hopeful signs of change, including the establishment of Britain's first women-led mosque in Bradford and the strong contribution by women in designing the UK's first 'eco-mosque' in Cambridge.

Campaigns like these to provide Muslim women with equal space to men are damaged rather than boosted by media and political scare campaigns against gender-segregated Muslim student events. Furthermore, the representation of Muslim gender segregation as an oppressive and extremist social practice ignores the ongoing and heated debates about gender segregation (in particular with regard to prisons and bathrooms) as it affects transgendered persons. Under the Trump presidency, Obama-era guidelines instructing schools to allow students access to the bathrooms and locker rooms that matched their gender identity were repealed. And at far-right rallies that I witnessed in Australia, the same speakers who were denouncing Muslims for their regressive gender norms denounced the Safe Schools Program (an initiative intended to support same-sex attracted, gender-diverse and intersex students) as a danger to 'our' children and values. And, even among feminists, the issue of gender identity and gender segregation is far from resolved, with bitter disputes over whether or not trans women ought to be permitted entry to designated female-only space.

Professor Sheila Jeffreys is one of the so-called TERFs (trans-exclusionary radical feminists) to have played a prominent role in both disputes. Jeffreys refuses to refer to transgender men and women by their preferred pronouns and regards attempts by transgender women to enter designated women's or lesbians' space as an intolerable masculine intrusion. British journalist Julie Bindel is similarly hostile to both Muslim men and transgender women. In 2017, Bindel was quoted by the *Daily Mail* as describing the decision to explicitly welcome transgender women to the popular women's only Hampstead Heath Ladies' Pond as 'totally unacceptable' and saying that 'the last thing [young girls] want is to look behind them and see some male-bodied person pretending to be a woman in order to gawp at them'.

Michigan Womyn's Music Festival (or Michfest) was a women's only music festival founded in 1976. As Michelle Goldberg describes in the *New Yorker*, Michfest provided an opportunity for audience members to not only enjoy performances by leading musicians, but also to experience life in a temporary matriarchy, with food cooked in communal kitchens, free childcare provided and the freedom to wear whatever they wanted (including nothing at all). But Michfest's refusal to admit transgender women led some of its scheduled performers to withdraw from the festival, while those who did attend had to run the gauntlet of the protest camp of trans supporters set up outside. These conflicts eventually led the organisers to disband Michfest in 2015.

Similar controversies have erupted in Australia, with organisers of the Victorian lesbian festival Lesfest denied an exemption from anti-discrimination in order to specify that the event was open only to 'female-born lesbians'. 'Lesfest 2004 is not for all lesbians – it is for those who identify as lesbians born female. Lesbians born female respect the right of all other groups to meet amongst themselves for their own reasons, and trust that they will be extended the same respect in return.' Another controversy took place in Adelaide a few years later, when a transgender woman fought an unsuccessful three-year battle for the right to accompany her partner to a lesbian event, Sappho's Party.

I was unaware of these disputes until I was asked at late notice to talk about issues affecting Muslim women at a feminist conference in Melbourne. Unbeknownst to me, the organisers of this event had split over the decision to include Sheila Jeffreys on the programme. Jeffreys eventually withdrew after being scheduled to appear on a panel alongside a transgender man. Her supporters picketed the conference opening and held a rival event nearby, at which Jeffreys was reported to have 'dedicate[d] her entire speech to vilifying transgender and transsexual people'.

The raw nerves that had been exposed by this disagreement were still on display during the conference itself. I was more than used to having my feminist credentials angrily disputed on the basis of my ethno-religious identity, but, for those concerned, the blows inflicted by this falling-out among those who had once regarded themselves as allies, or at least potential allies, had struck far closer to home than anything that I was likely to say or could ever do. For once, 'the Muslim issue' was one of the least contentious issues on the agenda.

Similarly, while Sheila Jeffreys' opinions on Islam as expressed in her book on religion and in her comments about gender-segregated student events caused great anger among many young Muslims, it was the response to her book on transgender identity that reportedly led the University of Melbourne to provide her with additional security and remove her name from her office door. Glitter-bombing, a form of protest more usually directed at public figures associated with homophobia, has recently been directed at feminists accused of transphobia as well. Germaine Greer was glitter-bombed at a public event in New Zealand in 2011 for her history of opposing the appointment of a transgender woman to her Oxford women's college. An unrepentant Greer remarked in 2015 that 'I didn't know there was such a thing [as transphobia]. Arachnophobia, yes. Transphobia, no.' Sheila Jeffreys says that she escaped being glitter-bombed after protesters arrived at one of her lectures on the wrong day.

Outside the feminist and LGBT networks concerned, these heated debates were widely regarded as fringe events, if not freak shows. Predictably, conservative men enjoyed the spectacle of feminists accusing each other of discrimi-nation. Sheila Jeffreys received support from Melbourne-based journalist and broadcast commentator Andrew Bolt both for her stance on transgender surgery on children and for her opposition to gender-segregated Muslim student events on campus. Quoting her response to the controversy over events at the University of Melbourne, he commented 'One Leftist, at least, is consistent in her beliefs.' Strange to find that, for at least one conservative male columnist, the only good feminist is a lesbian hard-line radical feminist. Although gender-segregated seating arrangements at a Muslim student event are represented as an us-versus-them clash of civilisations, feminists themselves are yet to agree on an issue as fundamental as who is and is not entitled to be considered a woman at all.

The assumption that is there a clear conservative consensus on the issue of gender identity among Muslims is equally simplistic. In his book *Sexual and Gender Diversity in the Muslim World: History, Law and Vernacular Knowledge*, Vanja Hamzić documents the ways in which sexually and gender-diverse Muslims have navigated Islamic law and social attitudes. Pakistan has offered a Third Gender option on the national ID card since 2012, with often heated debates between those who identify as transgender women and those who reject this identity in favour of the traditional designation of *Khawajha Sira*, or Third Gender. Iran, by contrast, has chosen to affirm a binary understanding of gender by providing state-funded access to gender-reassignment surgery and hormone replacement therapy for those who identify as trans, in line with a 1986 fatwa from the Ayatollah Khomeini – a cleric not known for his liberal attitudes to gender norms. However, this provides the Iranian state with a medicalised 'solution' to gender diversity, intended to corral sexually and gender-diverse people into heterosexual relationships.

The concept of a clear ideological divide between an inclusive West and a regressive and dangerous Islam over the issue of gender boundaries and identity dissolves upon closer examination. However, the proxy war over Islam and gender segregation has nonetheless served its purpose in marking out the ideological frontier between Muslim and Western values.

Problematic Alliances

Unfortunately, feminist anti-imperialists and anti-racists have on occasion taken a similarly with-us-or-against-us attitude – and ended up allied with socially conservative Muslim men. Code Pink is a US-based 'women-initiated grassroots peace and social justice movement working to end US-funded wars and occupations, to challenge militarism globally, and to redirect our resources into health care, education, green jobs and other life-affirming activities'. As part of its campaign against US militarism, members of Code Pink travelled to Pakistan in early October 2012 as part of a delegation of international peace activists who joined former cricketer and politician Imran Khan's 'peace march' to protest against drone attacks. In an unfortunate accident of timing, the delegation's day-long fast outside the Islamabad press club 'to atone for drone strikes' took place on the same day as the Taliban's shooting of Malala Yousafzai, which Khan so pointedly refused to blame on the Taliban (see Chapter 2).

Members of Code Pink later joined a protest against the attack on Malala outside the Islamabad press club and offered a $1,000 donation to her school. Importantly, they also noted that the Taliban had claimed responsibility for the shooting, which Imran Khan had failed to do. However, this did not assuage the anger of those feminists (both Pakistani and non-Pakistani) who condemned Code Pink's decision to link their campaign to Khan's in the first place.

As Malala's story became more prominent, left-wing opponents of the ongoing War on Terror began to critique the way that her case was being utilised as a moral alibi for US imperialism. However, this response was insufficiently alert to the ways in which it echoed the complex web of vilification, conspiracy theory and cognitive dissonance surrounding her story within Pakistan. Such critiques are always preceded by the acknowledgement that Malala is an immensely courageous young woman and that shooting her in the head was wrong. However, this caveat, too, reflects the rhetoric of some of Malala's most strident opponents, who are capable of damning and praising her in the same breath. Even Taliban spokesman Adnan Rashid sent his regrets, saying that he wished the attack had never happened and advising Malala to return to Pakistan and join a female madrassa near her home town.

As prominent Pakistani nuclear physicist and political commentator Pervez Hoodbhoy said, 'Unsurprisingly, leftist critiques of Malala's Nobel have been eagerly seized upon by right-wingers in Pakistan, helping seal the narrative for many of my countrymen and women.' Chetan Bhatt points out that Code Pink failed to mention the large number of 'enforced disappearances' in Baluchistan, which were a major concern to Pakistani human rights organisations at the time. Does our need to critique Western imperialism and Islamophobia short-circuit our ability to express appropriate solidarity with women and girls suffering violence at the hands of patriarchs who claim to be religiously inspired?

Code Pink's blunder was repeated in microcosm by anti-racism activists in Australia who allied themselves with conservative Muslim male leaders, often at the expense of Muslim women and much to our frustration. This was often due to the preparedness of many white anti-racists to accept the ways in which these Muslim leaders located us as less culturally loyal but also because of their willingness to subscribe to preconceived stereotypes of socially conservative authenticity.

Malala herself welcomed the news of Imran Khan's 2018 election victory, tweeting a statement in which she offered her congratulations and noted that Khan's party had nominated education as one of its top priorities. 'My hope is that Pakistan will someday be known as a global leader in education, a country where all children receive the schooling they need to pursue their dreams and contribute to their nation. I believe this can begin with this government and I hope to work with Prime Minister Imran Khan toward this noble goal.' This pragmatic willingness to let bygones be bygones is understandable for an activist whose foundation continues to operate in the nation now governed by Khan's party. However, this does not absolve activists from outside Pakistan for the failures that led them to focus on the casualties of US drone attacks (which Malala herself had also denounced) to the almost entire exclusion of the victims of Taliban violence.

Islamic/Muslim Feminism

Muslim women are the target of relentless demands to denounce various forms of gender violence – forced marriage, honour killing, but perhaps most of all female genital mutilation. These racialised denunciations of gendered violence are demanded by self-appointed saviours as well as hate-mongers. And if we fail in our responsibility to other Muslim women, if we are not sufficiently unambiguous in our denunciations of the crimes committed against them, then we have reinforced the need for other women (and men) to act in our place. The script for these denunciations is already set out, riding roughshod over the work of women from within those relevant communities who had already laid the groundwork for this enterprise. This has material consequences, as government welfare services are increasingly outsourced to external agencies and Muslim women's community groups are sidelined in favour of liberal feminist and sometimes Christian service providers who are prepared to state their mission in more uncompromisingly femonationalist terms.

These demands ignore the growing number of Muslim women scholars, activists and movements who are challenging the moral authority of Islamist patriarchy by grounding their discussion on women's rights on a religious foundation. They dispute the basis of discriminatory laws and social practices by questioning the extent to which they can truly be regarded as 'Islamic', and they offer alternative and (they maintain) more authentic interpretations of the Qur'an and other foundational Islamic texts that are consistent with the principles of gender equity. For example, the Malaysian NGO Sisters in Islam describes its mission as 'to promote the qualities of gender equality, justice freedom and dignity in Islam and empower women to be advocates for change'. Similar religiously defined organisations have arisen across the Muslim world, many of them focused on developing women's religious scholarship and breaking the masculinist monopoly on the interpretation of Islamic texts.

The term 'Islamic feminism' came into circulation in the 1990s, initially among scholars of Middle Eastern gender studies, before entering into more widespread use. As a concept, it holds many attractions, suggesting as it does that feminism is not the sole preserve of Western women and that Muslim women, too, have access to a history and a discourse of women's rights. However, this creates new questions and problems, and does not fully resolve the old ones. The term is highly contested, not least by some of the women who have been cited as its practitioners. It is often seen as having been imposed on its subjects by outsiders – non-Muslim feminist scholars based in the West who (in the words of Lila Abou-Bakr in 2001) use the term to 'categorise, label and name Muslim women'. However, one such scholar, Margot Badran, writes that she originally encountered the term in the work of Iranian women, and more and more Muslim women have adopted the term with regard to their own work. Even some of those, such as Asma Barlas, who do not accept the designated term of feminist have nonetheless engaged in productive conversations within the Islamic feminist framework.

Islamic feminists hold a very diverse range of theological and political worldviews, ranging from broadly left-liberal to the unapologetically right-wing imperial feminism of journalist Asra Nomani, who isolated herself from most of her coreligionists with an opinion article for the *Washington Post* headlined 'I'm a Muslim, a woman, and an immigrant: I voted for Trump', in which she cited the high cost of Obamacare and the Democrats' supposed reluctance to acknowledge the 'Islam' in 'ISIS'.

Margot Badran defines Islamic feminism as 'a feminist discourse and practice that derives its understanding and mandate from the Qur'an, seeking rights and justice within the framework of gender equality for women and men in the totality of their existence'. However, for some secular Muslims, naming this enterprise as 'Islamic feminism' risks labelling as 'non-Islamic' those Muslim women engaged in non-theologically based forms of feminism. It is only a small step from being non-Islamic to 'unIslamic' – a highly dangerous term to carry in contemporary Muslim societies. To date, this risk has been limited by the fact that 'Islamic feminism' has itself been regarded as an alien force by religious conservatives (since they consider 'feminism' of any description to be a Western concept). However, the term is gaining more widespread use among Muslim women beyond academia and in so doing has become associated with a religiously validated cultural 'authenticity', at the expense of other forms of feminism.

As Val Moghadam summarised in her 2002 essay 'Islamic Feminism and Its Discontents: Toward a Resolution of the Debate', 'Islamic feminists and their expatriate academic supporters [critics argue] either consciously or unwittingly delegitimise secular trends and social forces.' Such critics claim that, by accepting the basic premise of using theology as the foundation for social norms, 'Islamic feminists' reinforce the patriarchal power structures that they claim to challenge. Female empowerment, it is claimed, requires the wholesale removal of religion from public life. Asma Barlas responds to these 'secular fundamentalists' (as she calls them) by challenging their claim that the patriarchal voice in which the Qur'an is written is intended as a prescriptive norm, rather than just a reflection of the time and place in which it was revealed.

Many of the long-standing tensions between secular and religious Muslim women's rights activists have been resolved through collaborations on shared issues of concern – most notably, the racism which is directed at all of these activists, as well as the balancing act which all must perform between those who regard them as insufficiently Muslim on the one hand and those for whom their religious identity invalidates their identity as feminists on the other.

Casualties of the Proxy War

For those Muslim proxies who are seen as having passed their use-by date, the fall from grace can be swift and savage. Until 2017, Yassmin Abdel-Magied fell squarely on the 'good' side of the good-Muslim, bad-Muslim dichotomy. The gifted young Sudanese-born mechanical engineer was awarded the title of Queensland Young Australian of the Year in 2015 in recognition of her role as a social advocate and the co-founder of Youth Without Borders (an organisation for which my own daughter volunteered). Articulate, draped in a particularly glamorous array of hijabs and almost relentlessly optimistic,

Abdel-Magied was fulsome in her praise of Australia and a natural host of the Australian Broadcasting Corporation's 'Australia Wide' television show in which she presented 'stories from the people and places that make up the Australian experience'. Reflecting on her attitude at the time in an article for *Teen Vogue* in September 2017, Abdel-Magied said: 'I thought if I were good enough, my example would make people see that their assumptions about Muslims and people of colour were wrong. Once they got to know me, they would change their behavior and fix their biases, I thought.'

Abdel-Magied found herself at the heart of a political firestorm after her appearance on the Australian Broadcasting Corporation's panel show *Q&A* alongside right-wing independent Senator Jacquie Lambie. *Q&A* is known for its combative debates and the clash between Abdel-Magied and Lambie was no exception. To Lambie's line that there was 'only one law in this country and that is the Australian law' and that anyone who supports sharia law should be deported from Australia, Abdel-Magied responded, 'The fact is, sharia says that you follow the law of the land that you are on.' On women's rights, Abdel-Magied proclaimed: 'Islam to me is the most feminist religion. We got equal rights well before the Europeans.'

Aside from the substance of their respective opinions, this incident provided a lively spectacle in the form of a confrontation between a rough-around-the-edges working-class single mother who had entered Parliament as a representative of the underdog versus a well-educated, high-achieving migrant who was arrogant enough to believe that she could be an (in her own words) 'uber-patriotic Aussie' – and a feminist at that – while wearing a headscarf.

Abdel-Magied was ridiculed on both social and main-stream media for her assertion that Islam was a feminist religion, with a long list of abusive regimes and cultural practices cited as evidence against her. She was also attacked as an opportunist for a Department of Foreign Affairs and Trade tour of the Middle East she had under-taken, with the stated aim of 'showcas[ing] Australia as an open, democratic and diverse society in which Muslims are free to practise their faith'. This was described as a taxpayer-funded book tour on which Abdel-Magied, the self-described feminist, had failed to speak up for the rights of women in the region. A widely circulated cartoon from the national newspaper *The Australian* depicted her crouched next to a woman who is buried up to her neck waiting to be stoned, forcing the woman's mouth into a smile and declaring 'Selfie!' And an editorial by Ayaan Hirsi Ali in the same newspaper declared that Abdel-Magied's exchange with Jacquie Lambie had 'exposed [her] as a closet Islamist, in this case sympathetic to sharia law'.

A few months later, on Anzac Day (the day on which Australia and New Zealand commemorate their war dead), Abdel-Magied posted a tweet reading:

LEST. WE. FORGET.
(Manus, Nauru, Syria, Palestine . . .)

Manus and Nauru were references to Australia's offshore detention centres for asylum-seekers who enter Australian territorial waters by boat, while Syrian and Palestine of course referred to the bloody conflicts under way in those locations. Abdel-Magied deleted the tweet only a few hours later and apologised after a friend told her that it might be regarded as disrespectful to the nation's war veterans. But the fuse had already been lit, with an estimated 64,000 words written about her by media outlets and government politicians lining up to suggest 'self-deportation'. Her show on ABC television was not renewed (although she continues to make frequent appearances on the network) and the engineering company that had been her primary employer similarly declined to renew her contract. Only months after her notorious tweet, Abdel-Magied left the country to live in London, describing herself as having become 'Australia's most publicly hated Muslim'.

Abdel-Magied's experience illustrates the narrow role that femonationalism assigns to Muslim women who might otherwise endorse many of its core tenets. The furore that erupted around her served as a proxy war for debates on issues including the role of the publicly funded broadcaster that had hosted her show, increased diversity in Australian media, and shifting attitudes towards the commemoration of ANZAC history. Abdel-Magied was welcome to identify as feminist, but only if she took care to denounce Muslim misogyny wherever it was to be found. She was permitted to endorse national mythology, but not to appropriate it in order to highlight injustices primarily faced by members of her own global religious community. Having failed to meet these standards, she was ultimately more useful as a scapegoat than as a spokesperson.

And, as always, the major protagonists in this battle suffered far less damage than did the proxy.

5

INVISIBLE MENACE

In a matter of years, Europe as we know it will cease to exist.
    – 'Muslim Demographics', YouTube, March 2009

As for the policy of birth control, it is a disease that was injected into our fertile umma *by the enemy in order to decrease the Muslim population and weaken its strength.*
                                    – Rumiyah, 2017

Muslim women living in the West have long been regarded as a source of disruption to public space and, as illustrated by incidents such as by the burqas-in-Parliament debacle in Australia and the attempt to ban the burqini as a response to the terrorist attack in Nice, a potential threat to public safety. Scare campaigns targeting them most commonly focus on their visible presentation and behaviour, in particular, of course, the manner in which they dress. However, moral panics over Muslims as a demographic threat and over halal certification as a means of imposing sharia law have seen this type of scrutiny extended to the most intimate of private spaces – the content of their wombs and their stomachs.

Campaigns to regulate the wearing of hijabs and burqas in the West are part of a larger pattern in which public displays of religiosity by Muslims are regarded as an unwelcome disruption to the familiar landscape. Applications to build mosques in towns and suburbs across Europe, North America and Australia are routinely greeted with protests claiming that their construction would destroy the quality of life enjoyed by non-Muslim residents. A 2009 referendum in Switzerland voted to ban the construction of minarets, while in France Muslims are prohibited by law from praying on the streets after a campaign fanned by the leader of the far-right French Front National, Marine Le Pen, who described the practice as akin to the Nazi wartime occupation.

Those who express disapproval of public displays of religiosity usually concede that what Muslims do in their own homes and (approved) religious centres is their own private business. Muslims banned from praying on the streets of Paris were provided with temporary rented space in a disused fire barracks where they could worship out of sight of those non-Muslims who might otherwise feel that their country had been invaded. Similarly, Muslim women are regularly told that they should confine the use of hijabs and burqas to their private space – a directive that ignores the fact that veiling is practised in order to navigate public space and is regarded as unnecessary at home.

But, of course, that which is undertaken in private may be regarded as even more sinister and dangerous than practices performed in plain view where everyone can see what's going on. The scare campaigns over halal certification and Muslim demographics illustrate a shift in the representation of Muslims from a visible, alien presence to a hidden, covert threat. Anti-Muslim fearmongering increasingly focuses not on the danger of conquest by armed force, but on the use of 'stealth jihad' – the Islamisation of non-Muslim societies via peaceful means, undertaken so discreetly that the vanquished do not even notice their defeat.

As philosopher Martha Nussbaum has noted, Muslims are displacing Jews in the role of the hidden enemy within Western societies, and are regarded as all the more repulsive for their ability to conceal their true agenda. While the covert Jewish agenda was outlined in the notorious anti-Semitic hoax *The Protocols of the Elders of Zion*, the supposed Muslim conspiracy has been propagated in newspaper op-ed and media broadcasts, statements from politicians and a plethora of social media posts. An entire lexicon has been established around the theme of Muslim deceptiveness, with terms such as 'creeping sharia' and 'taqiyya' (the supposed doctrinal obligation for Muslims to lie to non-Muslims to advance the interests of their religious community) migrating from right-wing blogs and into the vocabulary of mainstream media outlets and politicians. As Arun Kundnani notes in his 2014 book *The Muslims are Coming! Islamophobia, Extremism and the Domestic War on Terror,* according to this worldview, '[t]he provision of halal food, shari'a compliant finance, or prayer breaks in workplaces is creeping shari'a, the first steps toward a society ruled by Islam'.

Western societies such as Australia, then, are being slowly poisoned from within as part of a cunning Muslim conspiracy – and poison has a reputation as the female criminal's weapon of choice.

At Home and Away

Feminist scholars such as Susan Moller Okin and Carole Pateman, working in the United States and the United Kingdom respectively, have unsettled the taken-for-granted status of the public/private dichotomy, in which 'masculine' public space is granted higher status than 'feminine' private space – with men holding ultimate authority in both spaces. And feminists have long campaigned for greater recognition of the fact that, since private space is the location where the abuse of women and children most commonly takes place, events and relationships that take place in private may therefore be an issue of legitimate public concern. Private space is regulated by rules established within the public domain, as lesbian, gay, bisexual and transgender (LGBT) campaigners know all too well. While contemporary attitudes have become less accepting of state intrusion into private space in order to regulate sexual conduct, it is increasingly accepted as legitimate for the purpose of combating violence against women and children.

Despite the continued prevalence of family violence across all segments of society, violence within Muslim homes is represented in highly racialised terms with a focus on practices such as forced marriage and female genital mutilation. Many commentators also claim that Muslim women only engage in public displays of piety because of patriarchal control wielded from the shelter of their male-dominated private space. British journalist Yasmin Alibhai-Brown tells the story of a young Muslim woman who introduced herself before removing her face-veil to reveal that she was 'so badly battered that she looked as though she had been beaten in deep blue, purple and livid pink'. Her father and brothers had bashed her as punishment for supposedly talking to an unrelated male. 'Then they forced me to wear the niqab, so no-one can see what they've done.'

Alibhai-Brown delivered 'Sara' (as she calls her) to a women's refuge, from where she eventually managed to build herself an independent, safe life. For Alibhai-Brown, Sara's story provides a compelling reason to ban face-veiling in order to prevent abusive men from using it as a means to conceal their crime. But Alibhai-Brown did not meet Sara until she had already made the decision to leave. For most victims of abuse, reaching this dangerous stage of their relationship is the most difficult challenge. Until that point, they are prepared to conceal the evidence of their injuries using cosmetics, clothing or elaborate explanations as to how they came about. There is no reason to believe that a ban on the burqa would protect women in Sara's situation from the family's violence. Rather, it allowed her to escape the confines of the home in which that violence took place.

Burqas disrupt the boundary between public and private space by providing a means to exercise privacy in the public arena. Lila Abu-Lughod, professor of Anthropology and Women's and Gender Studies at Columbia University, uses anthropologist Hanna Papanek's description of the burqa as 'portable seclusion' to describe the way it enables women to move out of segregated living spaces while still maintaining a barrier between themselves and unrelated men.

Since private space is held to be their prison, it follows, then, that Muslim women who are urged to enter public space do so in defiance of what are assumed to be their religious constraints. But their conduct in private space is regarded as potentially dangerous to the overarching public space in which it is embedded. Private space is secret, concealed – who knows what transgressive conduct may be undertaken there?

Halal, the Secret Ingredient

On Easter Saturday 2015, I attended a rally in Melbourne's Federation Square – one of sixteen 'Reclaim Australia' rallies held across Australia to protest against 'halal tax, sharia law and Islamisation'. Placards proclaimed slogans such as 'Islam is the enemy of the West', 'Halal is Sharia law' and 'Reclaim food free of sharia'. When I asked Reclaim Australia supporters what they meant by their 'Stop sharia law!' slogan, they cited beheadings and burqas but also angrily complained that sharia was 'in our food' because of halal certification. 'It's hidden inside the cheese packet – you can't see it until you open it!' In less than six months, a movement that had come to public attention via its Facebook campaign was featured in the lead story, as Reclaim Australia supporters clashed with anti-racist protesters in what John Elder, a senior correspondent with *The Age*, described as 'trench warfare'.

Halal as well as kosher food had attracted negative attention in the past on the grounds of alleged cruelty in slaughter practices, with animal welfare often a transparent pretext for racism. However, the moral panic that rose to prominence in 2014 focused not on cruelty against animals but on the halal certification of grocery items such as dairy, baked goods and cleaning products. Companies may obtain halal certification for their products by paying a fee to have it inspected by one of several Islamic authorities to establish that it does not contain forbidden ingredients such as pork derivatives or alcohol. Anti-halal campaigners (mirroring white supremacist campaigns against the so-called 'kosher nostra scam') describe this as a 'tax' on non-Muslim consumers, who are forced to subsidise Islamic religious practices. Worse still, the 'halal tax' may be used to fund terrorist attacks both in Australia and internationally. This scare campaign had been under way for some time on social media in Australia before gathering momentum to the point of being widely reported by mainstream media in October 2014.

Statements from the businesses concerned explained that the costs of halal certification were not passed on to the consumer and that their motives for obtaining it were strictly commercial. Given that halal certification provides Australian companies with access to lucrative export markets, most major political leaders also declined to endorse the anti-halal campaign. However, expressions of concern from some government and cross-bench parliamentarians culminated in the calling of a Senate inquiry into the third-party certification of food in May 2015. The inquiry covered all certification schemes, including kosher certification and the Heart Foundation 'tick' of approval. But, just as the French ban on visible religious symbols in state schools prohibiting the wearing of Christian crosses, Sikh turbans and Jewish *kippah* was understood as primarily targeting the hijab, halal certification was widely understood to be the main target of the Senate inquiry into food certification.

The inquiry's report recommended the introduction of a government-led halal certification scheme to replace the existing piecemeal landscape of rival certifying bodies, but found that 'there is no direct link between halal certification in Australia and terrorism funding' and that it did not force non-Muslim Australians to participate in a religious ritual. However, this reassuring conclusion did little to mitigate the damage caused by the process of the inquiry, which provided far-right fearmongering with weeks of media coverage. Some of the submissions made to the inquiry were withheld from public release due to their discriminatory content.

Of course, halal food is consumed by Muslim men, women and children alike. However, given that it revolves around the purchase and consumption of food, the campaign to boycott halal products is, unsurprisingly, highly gendered. Kathleen Blee, sociology professor at the University of Pittsburgh, published a study of women in the organised hate movement in the United States which noted the important role played by women racists in strategically deploying their control of family consumption, including boycotting items certified as kosher. A similar role is exemplified by the most prominent figure in the Australian anti-halal certification campaign, Kirralie Smith. The founder of Halal Choices Australia, Smith is described in her biographical notes as 'first and foremost a wife and home-schooling mother of three who holds a Bachelor of Theology and a Diploma of Ministry'. In a lecture delivered at a conference for the far-right Q Society (self-described as 'Australia's leading Islam-critical organisation') and made available on YouTube, she describes how, after being alerted to the role played by halal-certified food in funding sharia law, she realised that 'As a wife and a mother of three who does the shopping, I thought I could do something. I could take some form of responsibility for what we bring into our household.' A banner photograph on her website shows an attractive young white woman standing before a grocery shelf as she reads the label of the product held in her hands – the embodiment of the ideal responsible female household consumer.

And, as feminist scholars such as Susan Bordo have highlighted, women are expected to exercise control over the products that enter their bodies as well as their home. In so doing, women are urged to deploy the same qualities of self-restraint and discipline in abstaining from halal-certified food as those needed for any other dietary regime

– and are tantalised by the possibility that they may reap a similar reward as a side-effect. A 'humorous' post circulated on the Boycott Halal in Australia Facebook page and other anti-halal certification websites showed a slender female torso encircled by a tape measure, under the slogan 'I LOST 4 KILO'S [sic] by saying NO to halal certified foods. Boycott Halal in Australia and watch the kilo's [sic] come off.' And in fact some of the apparently female participants in anti-halal discussions on social media claim to have achieved gratifying levels of weight-loss by eliminating this ideologically tainted food from their diets. Like the diets promoted by the weight-loss industry, boycotting halal-certified products has made them more mindful of their food consumption, reduced their intake of off-limits and 'suspect' processed food, and increased their intake of fresh, non-halal and incidentally healthier food. The Boycott Halal in Australia Facebook page proclaims:

> A new trend? The HCF DIET – HCF = Halal Certified Free!
>
> So many of us have seen the kilos come off since we have not bought halal certified products – BOYCOTT HALAL!
>
> Since starting my HCF diet (halal certified free) 2 months ago I have lost 11 kg. I know [sic] fit into these jeans I couldn't even pull over my hips let alone button up.

Abstaining from the consumption of halal-certified food, then, supposedly allows women to attain the ideal of a pure, slender body, untainted by the corruption of foreign signifiers. And, like other right-wing movements, including Islamist movements, the anti-halal lobby provides women with the opportunity to participate in public discussion through the performance of their roles as homemakers and guardians of domesticity. Muslim women are seldom directly referenced in this campaign, but are visible as the ghostly obverse to this idealised non-Muslim woman.

Halal certification is alleged to enable violent as well as stealth jihad by raising money for terrorist movements. As a notice on the 'Halal Choices' Facebook page warned: 'My 2 cents worth: Young men don't go to Syria to "become" radicalized, they go because they already ARE radicalized. Where did that happen? right here in Australia (or London, France, USA, most likely in a mosque. A mosque that funded by your everyday grocery purchases.' Similarly, in a blog post titled 'Terror in the Tucker Box', National Party federal MP George Christensen (who had earlier supported calls to ban the burqa) demanded to know: 'Are groceries in Australian trolleys funding a push for Sharia law, supporting jihad groups or even backing terrorist activity?'

When a gunman held staff and customers hostage at the Lindt Café in Sydney in December 2014, forcing them to hold up a black flag emblazoned with the *shahada* (the Islamic declaration of faith, initially misreported as being the ISIS flag) at the window, it was hardly surprising to find that anti-halal campaigners concluded the café had been targeted because it had refrained from obtaining halal certification.

A notice on the Halal Choices Facebook page pronounced:

> Lindt chocolate is a beacon for the non-halal move-ment. Not a coincidence this has been targeted. So HORRIFIC! Let's hope against hope they are not waiting for the world to be watching before they do something unspeakable. The flag is the boast of Islam. Trains and public transport are being shut down, build-ings evacuated.

Nadia el-Mouelhy, CEO of the Halal Certification Authority of Australia, was reported to have left the Lindt Café just before the outbreak of the siege and was interviewed by various media outlets as the tragedy unfolded (her pink hijab duly noted). Her presence in that location, at that time, was regarded as highly suspicious by Islamophobic websites which refused to believe that it could possibly be a coincidence. The notoriously anti-Muslim American writer Robert Spencer wrote for his Jihad Watch website: 'A representative of an organisation that is paid huge amounts of money by companies for halal certification leaves an establishment that refuses to pay just before that establishment is subjected to a violent, murderous attack.'

In contrast, during the siege itself el-Mouelhy was supported by members of the public outside the café in Martin Place when another member of the crowd, described by the *Daily Telegraph* as a 'crazed man', began chanting, 'There's no such thing as a moderate Muslim.'

Ms el-Mouelhy was tapped on the shoulder by a Sydney businessman who smiled at her and said, 'Don't worry about him darling.' In Brisbane, Rachael Jacobs, an academic, former Greens candidate and daughter of Indian migrants, felt a similar impulse to show support when she noticed a woman on her train slowly unpin her scarf as news of the siege broke. Jacobs wrote a Facebook post describing how she had thought that 'if I simply offered to walk her to her destination, that might help'. One of Jacobs' friends shared the story on social media, using the #illridewithyou hashtag. Within hours, the post had been retweeted 120,000 times as the post went viral in a show of support for Muslims in Australia during uncertain times.

Unfortunately, the 'crazed' voices of those who refuse to believe the retort of Muslims such as el-Mouelhy – 'I'm a moderate Muslim' – grew ever louder and more insistent in the wake of the siege. If social media provided an outlet for gestures of support such as #illridewithyou, it was also the space in which the organisers of Reclaim Australia claim to have laid the groundwork for their response to the same crisis.

Predictably, the scaremongering about halal-certified food has been accompanied by attempts to confront Muslims and Jews with food that is known to be forbidden to them. Such attacks of course have a very long history. After the expulsion of the Jewish and Muslim communities from Spain, the Inquisition monitored the *Conversos* and *Moriscos*, who had converted to Catholicism rather than emigrate to safer territory, for evidence of pork consumption to ensure that they were not secretly maintaining their former religious identities. This historical echo was not enough to deter various right-wing councils in France from their 2015 decision to ban school canteens from offering students an alternative option when pork was on the menu. Former president Nicolas Sarkozy vowed to make the policy nationwide if he were returned to power in 2017, saying that students who did not wish to consume pork could instead be provided with 'a double portion of chips'. The 'double portion of chips' line was widely mocked and Sarkozy failed to progress past the first round of voting for his party's nomination. However, the issue of pork on school menus did not end with the election of the centrist Emmanuel Macron in 2017. In 2018, the Front National mayor of Beaucaire ordered the town's schools to serve pork every Monday, with no substitute meal to be provided.

Pork has been similarly weaponised by the far right at street level. As Amikam Nachmani relates, in 2003 soup kitchens affiliated with far-right organisations in Belgium and France began providing the needy with servings of so-called 'Identity Soup' – *identity*, of course, meaning pork. Coffee, dessert and cheese were also provided 'but no pork soup, no dessert'. The French courts initially banned these kitchens on the grounds that they were inflaming racial tensions, but the ban was overturned by a judge who ruled that Jews and Muslims were not discriminated against by a programme that offered only food that they chose not to eat on religious grounds.

I encountered a similar exclusionary welfare initiative at an event that was billed as a 'Feed for the Homeless' in my home town of Melbourne one evening in 2016. Dressed in black combat jackets with Viking helmets and the Australian flag emblazoned on the back, four members of the Soldiers of Odin were distributing leaflets, cupcakes and soup – pork soup, of course. The Australian offshoot of a Finnish far-right organisation, the Soldiers of Odin's leaflets proclaimed their identity as 'Patriotic Australians, Protecting Our Citizens, Defending Our Streets, Our Culture & Our Great Country'. Speakers at a Reclaim Australia rally that I attended later that year in the outer Melbourne suburb of Melton gloatingly invited their supporters to join them for a barbecue in a nearby park – of course, with pork sausages as the main attraction.

Other stunts have been more overtly confrontational. A small group of protestors from the United Patriots Front roasted a pig on a spit during a 2015 demonstration outside the ABC studios in Melbourne after the highly publicised appearance by alleged terrorist sympathiser Zaky Mallah on live talk show *Q&A*. And in December 2016, someone planted bacon rashers on the prayer mats in the Bankstown hospital prayer room, while Christmas cards containing bacon were sent to Sydney's Lebanese Muslim Association.

Muslims attempted to minimise the impact of these incidents by pointing out that the perpetrators had a dispro-portionate faith in the repellent power of pork. Popular comedian Nazeem Hussain responded to the bacon-laced Christmas cards by tweeting 'BACON IS NOT CRYPTONITE (sp) TO MUSLIMS. WE LOVE PIGS. WE DON'T EAT THEM. PIG-EATERS ARE

CRYPTONITE TO PIGS'. The Lebanese Muslim Association posted photographs of the hate-laced Christmas cards, with the notice 'END OF YEAR SALE! A wonderful selection of used Christmas cards, sent to us by adoring fans. Contain colourful language and extra special bacon bits. Get in quick as this offer won't last!' And prominent Sydney lawyer and founder of the Islamophobia Register Mariam Veiszadeh (who had herself been the intended recipient of a parcel of rotting pork) tweeted: 'Insider Tip: Muslims really hate chocolate! So leave chocolate in our prayer rooms. It will really pee us off!'

It was less easy to be light-hearted about the carefully wrapped parcel left at the doorstep of the Centre Culturel Islamique de Québec during Ramadan in 2016. The clear cellophane wrapping, the blue and white rosettes and the card featuring the greeting 'Bon Appetit' and a pig in a centrefold-style pose did nothing to conceal the bloodied snout of the severed pig's head 'gift'. This particular incident became global news several months later when a gunman entered the same mosque and shot dead six worshippers in what was eventually determined to be an unrelated attack. United States President Donald Trump made no public comment on the Quebec massacre, although he was reported to have offered his condolences in a phone call to Canadian Prime Minister Justin Trudeau.

In contrast, Trump showed no such reticence in his response to the 2017 terrorist attack in Barcelona that killed thirteen people, instead responding with a tweet that praised pork as kryptonite against Muslims. 'Study what General Pershing did to terrorists when caught.

There was no more Radical Islamic Terrorism for 35 years!' – an apparent reference to a discredited claim that General John J. Pershing executed Moro insurgents with bullets dipped in pigs' blood during the Spanish-American war in the Philippines in 1927. This belief in the near-supernatural power of pork-laced bullets is a popular far-right trope, to the extent that in 2013 the *Huffington Post* reported that a company in Idaho was selling a line of ammunition called 'Jihawg Ammo', coated with pork fat and marketed as 'Peace Through Pork'. 'With Jihawg Ammo, you don't just kill an Islamist terrorist, you also send him to hell.'

Meanwhile in India, the sale and consumption of beef has become a sensitive political trigger since the election in 2014 of a Hindu nationalist BJP government under the premiership of Narendra Modi. The slaughter of cattle has been banned in eighteen states while the prohibition of beef is enforced by so-called *gau rakshaks* – militias whose self-proclaimed mission is to protect the national 'cow mother'. Low-caste Hindus, Christians but most of all Muslims have all been targets for attack by these vigilante brigades. Most of the victims of so-called cow-related violence (or *gautankwad*) are male but women and girls are not immune. Media outlets including the BBC and the *Hindustan Times* reported on a 2016 case in which a twenty-year-old Muslim woman and her fourteen-year-old cousin were allegedly gang-raped and four of their male relatives killed after they were accused of eating beef. The woman told the BBC that '[the accused men] said that we had eaten cow meat and that was why we were being disgraced [raped]'. As Snigdha Poonam writes in an essay for the literary journal *Granta*, 'The Hindu cowboy accords to the cow the holiest status in his imagination: of mother. It is his duty to protect her honour; it is his privilege to kill for her.'

Muslim Demographics

The viral YouTube video 'Muslim Demographics' warns the world to 'wake up' to the threat of Islamic conquest not through force of arms, but through higher birth rates. It opens with the message 'The world is changing ... the global culture that our children inherit will be vastly different than it is today. You are about to witness a report on the world's changing demographics.' A soundtrack of 'oriental' music and ominous drumming introduces a warning about the danger of demographic decline. 'As the population shrinks, so does the culture ... Yet the population of Europe is not declining. Why? Immigration. Islamic immigration.' A crescent moon appears superimposed over a map of Europe. 'The world is changing. It's time to wake up ... This is a call to action.'

Watching the 'Muslim Demographics' video, I was reminded of thoughts I'd had after walking the streets of south London with my three young cousins when I was in my early twenties. They were delightful, well-behaved children – I secretly enjoyed the idea that I might be mistaken for their mother. Those streets were not always friendly. Stephen Lawrence, a young black man, had been murdered nearby in 1993 and the walls carried graffiti urging people to 'Kill all blacks, Pakis'. I was used to racist micro-aggressions. But I noticed that there was a different quality to the hostility I faced when I had my young cousins in tow. This didn't make sense to me. Who could possibly object to the sight of laughing, happy children on their way to the shops or the playground?

But then I caught the muttered words 'too many', and understood. Three offspring is not very many, but I was young enough to give birth to several more. 'They're scared of my *uterus!*' I thought. My capacity for bringing more 'Asian' children into the world was a threat.

Muslim women are now accused not only of potentially concealing weapons under their garments, but of harbouring a yet more sinister weapon within their bodies – their wombs. Muslim communities in the West, particularly in Europe, have been represented as a demographic threat to the 'native population', with projected demographics or pseudo-demographics forecasting a 'Muslim takeover' through sheer force of numbers rather than arms. Despite having been widely debunked, alarmist forecasts continue to circulate through both mainstream and social media of non-Muslim Europeans reduced to a struggling minority as the countries of their citizenship and ancestral heritage are overwhelmed by a booming Muslim population. And, of course, it is the capacity and apparent willingness of Muslim women to make a priority of childbearing ahead of other life choices that would enable such a demographic conquest. Muslim women are therefore not only transmitters of a dangerous ideology but also repulsive breeders of the enemy horde.

Muslims and Reproductive Rights

Contrary to both the paranoid fantasies of the demographic fearmongers and the patriarchal impulses of some clerics and community leaders, Islamic theology does not forbid the use of contraception or early term abortion in most circumstances. As a booklet published by the Malaysian civil society organisation Sisters in Islam outlines, since no verse in the Qur'an forbids family planning, most Islamic legal theorists believe that it is permitted. This outlook is supported by various *hadith* (or sayings attributed to the Prophet) permitting the use of coitus interruptus to prevent pregnancy. In addition, most scholars believe that the *ruh* or soul does not enter the body of the foetus or embryo until some point between twelve and forty days after conception, thus permitting abortion under a range of conditions. While conflicting rulings have been made regarding the factors that would justify abortion, there is a consensus in placing the life of the mother ahead of the need to continue a dangerous pregnancy at any stage. Where legal and social prohibitions on reproductive rights exist, they are generally based on the fear that access to contraception and abortion would allow women to conceal the evidence of their sexual transgressions and/or the belief that family planning contradicts predestination rather than on a belief in the unborn child's right to life.

As is the case in most communities worldwide, Muslim women who do not bear children are widely deemed to have 'failed' to meet a core female duty to their spouses and communities. However, as Asma Barlas writes in her 2002 book *Believing Women in Islam: Unreading Patriarchal Interpretations of the Qur'an*, the Qur'an does not define women solely through their role as mothers. The Prophet's wife Ayesha is regarded as a role model for Muslim women, despite the fact that she was never a biological mother.

Given this wide degree of theological leeway in regard to reproductive practices, initiatives undertaken by governments in order to exercise control over family planning have often been regarded as unIslamic. For example, in their study of nineteenth-century Ottoman state policies towards abortion, Turkish researchers Tuba Demirci and Selçuk Somel describe how the modernising state came to regard demographics as a matter of national security and abortion as akin to undermining the state. This led the newly emerging state to promulgate laws far more restrictive than those imposed by religious authorities. 'A realm considered by religious tradition as part of the sacredness and intimacy of Muslim families was regulated – and some said profaned – by the state authority.'

Demography remains a volatile political issue in much of the Muslim world, particularly in locations such as Lebanon and Malaysia, both of which have been the site of bloody communal violence. Israel and Palestine, in particular, have been the site of demographic rivalry between Arabs and Jews since population numbers can be expected to play a role in determining the borders in any political settlement. Yasser Arafat exhorted Palestinian families to have twelve children – two for themselves and ten for the struggle. For a time, such natalist slogans seemed to have an impact, with Palestinian fertility rates remaining high (including among educated women) while others in the region were falling in response to higher educational and living standards. However, even Palestinian fertility has seen a decline since 2000, despite the continued importance of demographic rivalry in Arab–Israeli politics. According to demographist Youssef Courbage and anthropologist Emmanuel Todd, 'The high fertility rate of Israeli Arabs is a threat to the Jewish state, whereas the high fertility rate of the Jewish settlers threatens Palestinian predominance in the West Bank.' Muslim birth rates have also been the focus of panics by Hindu nationalists in India and by the Burmese government, which introduced a two-child limit for Rohingya Muslims in 2013 under the pretext that their high birth rates had been a trigger for violence between the country's Muslim and Buddhist communities.

However, in the view of Courbage and Todd, the range of fertility rates among Muslim women suggests that demographics are best explained by factors other than religion, since they conform so strongly to socio-economic patterns. Natalist and anti-natalist policies by the governments of some Muslim-majority societies such as Iran and Malaysia also fail to conform to a consistent template and have only partially outweighed the force of these underlying factors.

This of course has not prevented Muslim governments and leaders from attempting to impose their will upon women's reproductive decisions. Turkish President Recep Tayyip Erdoğan described birth control as 'treason' in a

2014 speech, while in 2016 he described women who rejected motherhood in order to focus on their careers as 'deficient' and 'incomplete'. Uglier still was an article in the ISIS online magazine *Rumiyah* which described birth control as 'a disease which was injected into our fertile *umma* by the enemy in order to decrease its number and weaken its strength'. Likewise, the article continued, 'we will not miss this opportunity to warn every Muslim sister of another evil policy of Islam's enemies, which is to delay marriage until a later age'. (Yet, according to a 2016 report in the *New York Times*, ISIS forced its female captives to take contraception in order to prevent pregnancy and ensure their availability for the purpose of rape.)

However, while the 2017 Pew Research Center report on the global Muslim population found that a combination of relatively higher birth rates and a young population is set to see Islam overtake Christianity as the world's largest religion in the second half of this century, total fertility rates in a range of Muslim-majority countries including Iran, Saudi Arabia, Indonesia and Bangladesh have declined steeply, while others such as Pakistan and Egypt with continued high birth rates are in transition towards stabilisation. A similar trend is under way in Muslim communities in Europe. The moral panic over Muslim birth rates, however, continues to boom.

Fertility as a Weapon?

'The myth of the Muslim tide', as journalist Doug Saunders describes it in the title of his 2011 book, was investigated by the 2016 IPSO MORI 'Perceptions of Reality' survey, which asked members of the public across forty countries about key global issues and features of the population of their country. One of the report's key findings was that the public perceptions across Europe, North America and Australia overestimate 'by a staggering amount' both their countries' current Muslim population and the rate at which it is growing.

As the notorious 'Muslim Demographics' YouTube video illustrates, Europe is regarded as the front line in the battle against Islamic demographic conquest. Where Muslims are seen as a demographic threat in Europe, the governments of many of the countries in question – including France, Germany and the Netherlands – do not include religious affiliation in census data or other government statistics. Current figures, let alone future demographic forecasts, rely on estimation based on country of origin at best and ideologically driven guesswork at worst. Most of the figures cited in the 'Muslim demographics' video are simply fabricated. As Oliver Hawkins, producer of a BBC radio programme on the subject, pointed out, if the video's statistics were true, it would mean that Muslim women in the Netherlands are reproducing at nineteen times the rate of their non-Muslim counterparts. And, as German researcher and author Riem Spielhaus notes in her discussion of the emergence of Muslims into German public discourse, analyses of Muslim demographics conflate ethnicity with religion, homogenise a diverse range of communities and assume that religious identity will be transmitted across generations. However, such complexities have done nothing to abate warnings that Muslim communities are under-taking a so-called 'third jihad', described by author Bruce Bawer as 'a demographic overpowering of Europe's native peoples'. And, of course, childbearing Muslim women are seen as the enablers in this demographic battleground.

The far-right obsession with Muslim demographics was violently manifested in Anders Breivik, the Norwegian terrorist who murdered seventy-seven people in twin attacks on government buildings in Oslo and on a Workers' Youth League Summer Camp in Utoya in July 2011. Breivik's so-called manifesto, titled *2083: A European Declaration of Independence*, was a compilation of writing from fringe right-wing writers such as Bat Ye'or, Robert Spencer and Pamela Geller, as well as more mainstream right-wing figures such as *Daily Mail* columnist Melanie Phillips and Australian historian Keith Windschuttle. And the alleged Muslim demographic threat played a central role in Breivik's manifesto, including in his explanation of its title. As Liz Fekete from the London-based Institute of Race Relations writes:

> Thus, in a footnote to *2083*, Breivik explained the signif-icance of the date 2083, which is 400 years since the last siege of Vienna by the Turks. He then went on to quote Henryk M Broder, who wrote that: 'After the defeats of Poitiers (732) and Vienna (1683), the Europeans are now defeated with the weapons of demography'.

Breivik expanded on this topic by including extracts from the writing of Bat Ye'or and Robert Spencer as well as authoritative-looking but fabricated tables of statistics. For Breivik, as well as for a range of mainstream published writers, this illustrated the emergence of 'Eurabia' – the Islamisation of Europe via a combination of immigration and high Muslim birth rates. For the demographic alarmists, this fulfils the threat apparently foreshadowed in a 1974 speech to the United Nations by the Algerian dictator Houari Boumedienne: 'One day, millions of men will leave the Southern Hemisphere to go to the Northern Hemisphere. And they will not go there as friends. Because they will go there to conquer it. And they will conquer it with their sons. The wombs of our women will give us victory.' As historian Keith Robbins notes, 'It was not a speech which was well-received in the Northern Hemisphere.'

Similarly badly received was a 2017 speech by Turkish President Erdoğan in which he expanded on his long-standing calls for Turkish women to bear more children by telling his Turkish 'brothers and sisters' living in Europe: 'Go live in better neighbourhoods. Drive the best cars. Live in the best houses. Make not three, but five children. Because you are the future of Europe. That will be the best response to the injustices against you.'

Fears around the size of Europe's Muslim population have of course been further fuelled by the recent influx of refugees migrating to Europe from conflict zones in Muslim-majority regions of the Middle East, Africa and Asia. Responding to those concerns, in November 2017 the Pew Research Center released a set of projections for the future size of Europe's Muslim population based on three different levels of migration. The report forecast that the Muslim share of Europe's population would continue to grow even if further migration were to immediately cease. However, even under a high migration scenario in which the Muslim population were to rise to 14 per cent, they would remain outnumbered by the populations of both Christians and people of no religion.

Muslim Population in Australia

In 2016, a group of Queensland gun enthusiasts attracted national headlines by posting on Facebook and YouTube a video depicting them shooting plush toys dressed in 'Middle Eastern' garb. Most of the effigies were males, with one presented as the 'grand Muffin' (an apparent caricature of the grand mufti), while another wore a towel on his head and was shown calling 'Allah, Allah, Allah'. Both were shot, exploding into a cloud of white stuffing. And Muslim women as well as men were the enemy in this ethnic cleansing puppet show. As the camera focuses on a female effigy wearing a headscarf, a male voice exclaims 'Shit! There's another one! A breeder!' – and then pulls the trigger.

Australian population fears have historically centred on a fear of under- rather than overpopulation. The rationale for this fear has shifted away from the fear of invasion from the north – the 'yellow peril' – and towards concerns about labour market needs and the burden of an ageing population. As economic journalist Christopher Jay wrote in a 2004 essay, Howard-era apprehensions about falling birth rates underlie both a raft of 'family friendly policies' and treasurer Peter Costello's memorable axiom that couples ought, if they could afford it, have 'one for mum, one for dad, and one for the country'.

Despite this, there is still a space for claims that Australia is already too highly populated for its fragile environment to sustain. The highest-profile claim is the campaign run by businessman Dick Smith, in which racial anxieties are clearly visible. As a 2010 article by Guy Pearse in *The Monthly* points out, Smith launched his $1 million 'Wilberforce Award' (named after the British anti-slavery campaigner) for a young Australian to communicate alternatives to what he claimed was our 'growth addiction' flanked by 'five inexplicably smiley "blonde bombshells" wearing T-shirts declaring "Constant Growth = Doom"'. His 'Dick Smith Population Puzzle' documentary broadcast on ABC1 showed footage of overcrowded slums in Bangladesh and warned that 'Australia is currently growing even faster than here'. In 2017, he returned to this cause, launching a million-dollar campaign which drew upon similar images of 'third world' poverty – calling for Australia's immigration intake to be halved – and inexplicably posing with a sickle for the launch of an advertisement based on a famous 1980s 'Grim Reaper' campaign warning about the dangers of AIDS.

Population growth in Australia is mostly due to immigration rather than birth rates and its population fears – including fears about the size of its Muslim population – centre on an obsessive preoccupation with unregulated migration. Concerns about Australia being 'overrun' by Muslims have focused on their roles as asylum-seekers, rather than as overly fertile breeders. And, as a settler-colonial society rather than a former imperial power, Australian dynamics in the area of immigration and population are very different from those of Europe. Australia is still dealing with the ongoing legacy of the notorious White Australia immigration policy rather than with the aftermath of Empire.

However, in Australia as in Europe, Muslim demographics are a target of particular fear. In a 2017 episode of the Australian Broadcasting Corporation panel show *Q&A*, an audience member asked a pre-approved question: 'In view of the fact that, in Australia, Muslim couples have a much higher birth rate than the rest of us, is it not possible that, in a couple of generations, Australia could have a Muslim majority who vote in Sharia law?'

This alarmist claim was quickly debunked by the studio guests and by a follow-up explainer in *The Conversation* by demographer Liz Allen. However, it reflected a widespread and resilient misconception. The 2014 survey by the UK-based Ipsos MORI Social Research Institute mentioned earlier found that Australians 'hugely overestimate the proportion of Muslims in Australia. We think that 18 per cent of the population is Muslim when the actual figure is 2 per cent.'

Exaggerated beliefs about the size of Australia's Muslim population are often paired with concerns about 'Muslim enclaves', where non-Muslims are supposedly at risk of being outnumbered by Muslims. Kevin Andrews, a senior Liberal MP and former immigration minister, addressed the topic of Muslim enclaves and population growth during an interview with radio broadcaster Alan Jones in 2009. 'To have a concentration of one ethnic or one particular group that remains in an enclave for a long period of time is not good.' On the issue of Muslim population levels, Andrews responded that it was a topic that needed to be discussed: 'It's ridiculous if you can't talk about any subject.' Other Coalition politicians quickly moved to distance themselves from this type of uncoded racial targeting.

No such restraint is shown by members of the increasingly visible Australian far right, who have adopted the language of their European ideological comrades. Mike Holt, CEO of Restore Australia, received national media coverage after appearing as one of the main speakers at a Reclaim Australia rally in Newcastle in April 2015. 'It seems to us that the Islamic people who've come over here don't integrate into society. Islam could eventually take over Australia not through terrorism or war, but simply by outbreeding us.'

Holt's thoughts on this issue are set out in greater length in a post on his 'Islam 4 Infidels' website. The post includes a link to the 'Muslim Demographics' YouTube film and shows a map of Sydney with particular suburbs highlighted:

This map shows what is going on in Sydney right now. The pink areas are either fully Islamised, or changing that way. Islamic mullahs come to Australia and preach that Muslims must outbreed us so that they can take over our nation. They will deny this, of course, but the evidence is out there in videos and the written word.

Of course, demographic fearmongering also taps into the imagined link between fertility and male virility. Halal Certification Authority director Mohamed El-Mouelhy managed to hit this nerve with a 2017 Facebook post in which he responded to media reports about declining male fertility in the West by stating (or according to the headline in the *Herald Sun* newspaper, 'taunting'):

> Australian women need us to fertilise them and keep them surrounded by Muslim babies while beer-swilling, cigarette smoking, drug injecting [sic] can only dream of what Muslim men are capable of. If the country is left to the bigots the white race will be extinct in another forty years. Muslims have a duty to make your women happy because you are declining, better choose a plot for yourself in the local cemetery.

After a predictable media and political furore, El-Mouelhy eventually told radio interviewer Chris Smith that his post was intended as 'tongue in cheek' to 'stir the bigots' who had deluged his Facebook page with Islamophobic comments after he lodged defamation proceedings against the founder of the Halal Choices website (in a case that was eventually settled out of court) and was not directed at white people in general. The 'bigots' (including tabloid newspaper columnists and politicians), however, were duly stirred by El-Mouelhy's misguided attempt at humour. And not just the bigots. Most of my Muslim female friends also failed to appreciate the 'joke'.

Take up the White Woman's Burden

If Muslim women are having too many babies, then non-Muslim women are having too few, selfishly focusing on their careers at the expense of their reproductive labour. Anxieties around women and demographics are twofold, focusing on both those (disproportionately ethnic and indigenous) women who are stigmatised for breeding too young and too often and those (disproportionately white) women who are stigmatised for breeding too late and too infrequently.

In her 2017 book *In the Name of Women's Rights: The Rise of Femonationalism*, Sara R. Farris describes how the gender policies of far-right parties such as Italy's LN and France's FN 'related to classical right-wing concerns for women's fertility rates'. Hence the support for pro-natalist policies such as Le Pen's proposal to encourage French women to have more than two children by providing generous family allowances to families with at least one French parent.

Similarly, the campaign by the far-right AfD for the 2017 German elections featured a poster that showed a smiling pregnant blonde woman lying in a park under the slogan 'Neue Deutsche? Machen wir selber' ('New Germans? We'll make them ourselves').

Australia's population and racial anxieties have played out in public and political expectations that white women ought to reduce the nation's reliance on immigration by fulfilling their reproductive duties. As academic and author Erica Millar writes, 'When people or practices are likened to floods threatening Australia's security, asylum-seekers, for example, present an external threat. Conversely, abortion threatens to erode the white nation from within.'

This claim was most explicitly expressed by Coalition backbencher Danna Vale during the 2006 parliamentary debates about providing access to the abortion treatment drug RU-486. In a press conference to launch the campaign against the new treatment, Vale announced:

> I have read ... comments by a certain imam from the Lakemba Mosque [who] actually said that Australia is going to be a Muslim nation in 50 years' time. I didn't believe him at the time. But ... look at the birthrates and you look at the fact that we are aborting ourselves almost out of existence by 100,000 abortions every year ... You multiply that by 50 years. That's 5 million potential Australians we won't have here.

Vale's Coalition colleagues, including some of those who shared her opposition to RU-486, distanced themselves from her anti-Muslim scaremongering. However, her views reflected a prominent public concern in claiming that 'mainstream' women had abandoned the domestic space, thus leaving it vulnerable to takeover by Muslim women spearheading an Islamic invasion of Australian society. As Erica Millar remarked, 'By excluding Muslim women from the category "Australian", and prescribing a particular role for non-Muslim (white) women – that of national breeders – Vale clearly claimed Australia as a nation that belonged to non-Muslim (implicitly white) bodies.'

Around the same time as the right-wing Reclaim Australia rallies were under way, police were reported to have launched but then 'quietly dropped' an investigation into a series of anonymous hate mails that were sent to a range of recipients. The letters were described as attacking Aboriginals and Muslims and warning against a coming 'demographic genocide'. Wombs, it turns out, can be at least as dangerous as bombs.

A Watching Brief on Fear

Some of the Muslim pushback against these fear campaigns has succeeded in gaining traction across the broader community as well. The Halal Snack Pack Appreciation Society was established during the height of the halal certification panic-mongering in 2016 as a Facebook tribute to the Styrofoam takeaway boxes of chips, kebab meat and a criss-cross of garlic and chilli sauce that had been available in Australian kebab shops for decades. The HSP (as it was dubbed) soon became a hot favourite in takeaway food outlets nationwide, with a vegan version on offer at the vegetarian Lord of the Fries chain. Announcing the term 'Halal Snack Pack' as the People's Choice for its 2016 Word of the Year, the *Macquarie Dictionary* committee described it as 'something once confined largely to the Muslim community that is now surfacing throughout the broader Australian community'.

Light-hearted responses like the HSP Appreciation Society have helped to minimise the impact of anti-Muslim scare campaigns. However, the moral panics around food and reproduction cannot simply be dismissed as a joke, given their ability to filter through to mainstream party politics and their potential to incite serious political violence such as the mass murder committed by Anders Breivik.

Muslim women are used to the idea that 'fitting into' the dominant culture can provide a means of minimising racist discrimination and harassment. However, Muslim identity has now become so racialised that private, invisible behaviour may be regarded as posing as much of a threat as public acts of perceived defiance. As Liz Fekete points out, Jean-Marie Le Pen, the former leader of the French Front National, refused to support proposals to ban the headscarf on the basis that wearing it made Muslim women easier to identify and monitor. And, as scaremongering on halal certification and Muslim demographics illustrates, there is no aspect of Muslim life so intimate that is not considered worthy of surveillance.

6

'JIHADI BRIDES' AND CHICKS WITH STICKS

Idiots that are tweeting this trend should realise that
NO SISTER ever leaves the comfort of their homes just
to marry some man.
      – @UMMWAQQAS, Twitter, 9 April 2015

Sex and death has always been a highly marketable combination, so it's hardly surprising that reports of so-called
'jihadi brides' have attracted such strong media interest:
young femmes fatales defying their parents and government authorities by running away to offer themselves as
wives and housekeepers in the service of the Islamic State
(also known as ISIS, ISIL or Daesh) – their black niqabs
providing the perfect screen upon which to project our
fantasies of the beautiful bad girl. With the fall of the self-
declared IS 'caliphate' in Syria and Iraq, reports of the
departure of young women from locations such as London

and Sydney have been replaced by accounts of their deaths, debates about who should bear responsibility for those who have survived and fears about the risk posed by those who have returned to the countries in which they had been raised or conversely by those who had been unable to leave.

In contrast to the 2003 speech delivered by George W. Bush on the aircraft carrier USS *Abraham Lincoln* beneath a banner reading 'Mission Accomplished', leaders and analysts are describing the conflict with IS as a 'generational struggle'. Governments are responding to this struggle with an apparently endless round of new security legislation and a string of initiatives to 'counter violent extremism' (or CVE) – a contentious strategy that seeks to enlist community organisations, educational institutions, service providers and individuals in promoting a model of good citizenship to Muslims and isolating not only those individuals and organisations who are suspected of undertaking a criminal offence, but also those who are regarded as 'at risk' of radicalisation and whose ideology is seen as aligning with extremism. And Muslim women are expected to play a key role in this struggle.

Muhajirat

There is no single template for the young women from North America, the United Kingdom, Europe and Australia who joined Islamic State. Much of the academic literature refers to them as 'migrants' in preference to the sensational and reductive 'jihadi bride' label, with Erin Saltman and Melanie Smith, authors of a report on gender and ISIS, noting that this is the English translation of the term *muhajirat* used by the women themselves. While some migrants such as Australian Tara Nettleton and Brit Sally Jones came from the societal margins, others were high achievers who seemed set for a bright future prior to their abrupt departure for Syria. Many of the young recruits do not come from particularly religious families, while a few are (or were) converts who reportedly connected with their IS recruiters online.

In response to a question in Parliament in February 2015 about how the Australian government planned to prevent young Australian women from leaving the country to participate in the conflict in Iraq and Syria, then-Foreign Minister Julie Bishop told Parliament:

Yet more women are either joining their foreign fighter husbands or apparently seeking to find partners – the so-called jihadi brides – or are otherwise providing support for terrorist organisations. Some are joining all-female groupings, which impose Daesh's sick and misguided doctrine on other women in Daesh-controlled areas. According to estimates, women now account for nearly one-fifth of all foreign fighters. Over 500 women are believed to have come from Western countries. Thirty to 40 Australian women are known to be either engaging in or supporting terrorist activity in Syria, Iraq and here in Australia.

This defies logic given we know the attitude of Daesh towards women. If the killings and executions are not enough, Daesh has published instructions on the treatment of sexual slaves, which includes raping and beating women. Even children are not immune, with instructions encouraging sexual assault on girls who have not yet reached puberty.

Julie Bishop is far from alone in regarding female support for ISIS as 'defying logic'. Muslims and non-Muslims alike struggle to comprehend these young women and the lives they have chosen. Their participation is one of the many apparent contradictions that make ISIS appear bizarre and novel – a regime that is brutally patriarchal yet is able to attract female recruits; a movement regarded by outsiders as a medieval throwback yet that is also an adept user of cyberspace. However, there are both historical precedents and contemporary parallels for all of ISIS's supposedly freakish characteristics. Placing ISIS in a wider geographic and longer historical context therefore reveals many familiar resonances.

The advent of ISIS has further underscored the binary between Good and Bad Muslim women, between 'moderates' and 'extremists'. As the Bad woman grows even badder, the role of the Good Muslim woman has become ever more crucial. Muslim women are no longer the helpless victims of their male relatives – they are powerful matriarchal figureheads who can stand between them and the battlefield. Good Muslim women are expected to convince their offspring to act as government informants – a dangerous role during times of tension.

And Bad Muslim women are not only those who themselves engage in violent or criminal acts. They are also those who have failed to exercise a sufficiently positive influence over their families, to have performed their religious identity in a manner that is fully compatible with 'our' values, to have instilled a robust ideological barricade against the hazards of violent extremism, to have undertaken the considerable labour that is required of the Good Muslim woman.

Chicks with Sticks

Women are usually regarded as victims of Islamist politics rather than participants. Media coverage of women Islamists tends to depict them as novel and anomalous – almost a contradiction in terms. Yet most Islamist parties have highly active women's wings, without which they could not have achieved popular acceptance. Islamist movements owe a great deal of their appeal to the success of their welfare programmes, which fill the gaps left by the failure of governments to provide adequate services in health, education and social services. In gender-segregated communities, such services could not operate effectively without the contribution of the women's wings, whose members are able to gain access to other women and to private homes.

For many mainstream Pakistan feminists, even non-violent initiatives 'defied logic' when undertaken by women on behalf of patriarchal ideologies and movements (see Chapter 2).

The participation of women and girls in the 2007 occupation of the Lal Masjid in Islamabad by militant clerics and students therefore came as a shock. Female students and staff from the Jamia Hafsa seminary attached to the mosque undertook a morals campaign that led the Pakistani media to dub them 'chicks with sticks', after the bamboo canes that they wielded on their patrols of the local neighbourhood. Amid heated debate about whether some or all of the women and girls were acting as autonomous agents, had fallen victim to a form of 'false consciousness', or were being held by force, the 'chicks' detained women whom they accused of running a brothel and created an international incident by raiding a Chinese-run massage parlour.

Raheel Qazi, the Jamaat-e-Islami leader whom I had interviewed years earlier, visited the besieged mosque in an attempt to negotiate the departure of the women and girls from the seminary, but was refused access by both the military and the mosque leadership. As she later told me:

> I spoke to the women inside but they also refuse to listen me because they believed at the time that we are the liberal ulema (religious scholar). So we are sandwich-like. We are moderate people, so the extremists also blame us, and the seculars also blame us. So I believe that I'm on the very middle of the path and I invite all the others to join me there for the peace and the love and the prosperity of this country.
>
> We condemn state terrorism, but terrorism and the terrorist groups – we condemn them also. We believe in education, we believe in dialogue, we believe in the rule of law.

The number of women and girls killed when the military eventually stormed the mosque remains contested.

And controversy surrounding the seminary continues. In 2014 Pakistani media reported that a 'distraught' father had joined the campaign against the Lal Masjid in an attempt to secure the return of his twenty-six-year-old daughter, who had left home in order to live at the seminary. He had appealed to the Supreme Court for help. And in 2016 the *Washington Post* gave an account of intelligence reports about a group of women and girls from the seminary apparently video-recording a pledge of allegiance to Islamic State.

Pakistanis have been even more riveted by the Pakistani neuroscientist Aafia Siddiqui, who is serving an eighty-six-year sentence in the United States after her conviction for attempting to kill US agents while being interrogated in Ghazni, Afghanistan, in 2008. Siddiqui holds enormous star power in Pakistan, where she is widely regarded as the innocent victim of a US conspiracy and where stories circulate about her alleged mistreatment while in prison. The US-trained neuroscientist disappeared along with her three children in 2003 after being placed on an FBI global alert list. In 2004 she became the only woman on a list of seven most-wanted al-Qaeda fugitives. US authorities claim that she was on the run with her al-Qaeda co-conspirators, until she reappeared in Afghanistan in 2008. She was taken into custody and supposedly managed to grab a rifle and fire upon her captors, shouting 'Death to America!' Her supporters, however, believe that either the Pakistani or the US authorities secretly detained her during those missing years.

No wonder, then, that ISIS should seek to associate itself with the brand of the woman whom US counter-intelligence officials had reportedly dubbed 'Lady al-Qaeda'. In 2014, ISIS offered to exchange the American journalist James Foley for her – an offer the United States unsurprisingly declined to pursue. After broadcasting Foley's execution, ISIS made a similar offer with regard to US-Israeli journalist Steven Sotloff, with a similarly gruesome outcome. Siddiqui's sister has disassociated the family's campaign for her release from the proposed deals, telling *Newsweek* that ISIS was just trying to capitalise on Aafia's cause.

ISIS then made an offer for the release of Sajida al-Rishawi, who was sentenced to death in Jordan after failing to detonate her explosive belt during a 2005 triple-bombing attack in Amman that killed sixty people. Al-Rishawi lacked Siddiqui's glamour, but, on the other hand, as the reported sister of a close aide to Abu Musab al-Zarqawi, she had an impeccable al-Qaeda pedigree. In 2005, she and her husband travelled from Iraq to Jordan in order to participate in a coordinated attack on three separate hotels in Amman. When her bomb failed to detonate, her husband pushed her back out of harm's way before detonating his own device, killing thirty-eight wedding guests. ISIS demanded her release, first in exchange for Japanese journalist Kenji Goto and then for Jordanian pilot First Lieutenant Moaz al-Kasasbeh (whom Jordanian officials believe was probably already dead).

'Jordan's response will be earth-shattering,' said Jordan's information minister after ISIS eventually released the now-notorious video showing al-Kasasbeh's execution by fire. Hours later, the most obvious prime target for revenge, Sajida al-Rishawi, was hanged in Jordan alongside convicted al-Qaeda operative Ziyad Karboli. But al-Rishawi's execution may have served ISIS's purposes at least as well as her release could ever have done. Analysts note that the escalated use of female suicide bombers is in large part due to the high volume of media coverage they attract in comparison to their male counterparts. In this regard, al-Rishawi's 'failed' suicide bombing comes as a spectacular success. Her martyrdom came nearly a decade later than originally planned, but in public relations terms it has achieved more than she and her co-conspirators had ever dared hope.

And, given al-Rishawi's close association with al-Qaeda, this public relations exercise was directed not just at the US government, but also at the rival jihadi organisation from which ISIS had symbolically poached her.

Home-Grown Extremists

Cases of so-called 'home-grown' Muslim women extremists in the West prior to the rise of ISIS include that of Samina Malik, who described herself as a 'lyrical terrorist' and wrote poetry in celebration of beheadings. Her conviction in 2008 as the first woman found guilty under the United Kingdom's newly introduced anti-terrorism laws was eventually overturned. In 2010 Roshonara Choudhry, a young British woman, stabbed Labour MP Stephen Timms after 'self-radicalising' under the influence of Islamist websites. She later said that she attacked him because he had voted to send British troops into Iraq. In Australia, Rabiah Hutchinson, described in media reports as 'the girl from Mudgee', had converted to Islam as a student and was married to a member of al-Qaeda's governing council. Hutchinson, who was running a women's health clinic in Taliban-controlled Afghanistan at the time of the 9/11 attacks, had her passport confiscated by the Australian authorities and was placed under surveillance by the Australian Security Intelligence Organisation (ASIO).

However, none of these earlier cases had carried the sensational impact of the stories about a wave of women and girls absconding from various locations in the West to marry the jihadi warrior of their cyberdreams in the killing fields of Syria and Iraq. Among those to have 'defied logic' (in Julie Bishop's words) by leaving their secure homes in the West in order to join the so-called Islamic State are Aqsa Mahmood, the 'former private schoolgirl' from Glasgow who has now been stripped of her British citizenship for her alleged role in enticing other young women and girls to Syria; the sixteen-year-old twin sisters Salma and Zahra Halane from Manchester in northern England; and Gold Coast-raised Amira Karroum from Australia, who was executed alongside her Adelaide-born husband just two days after her arrival in Syria where they had reportedly joined ISIS's rival Jabhat al-Nusra.

The social media accounts of these young female migrants (most of which have now been shifted to less public platforms or been taken offline) were mined for information about their possible motives. How can a young woman tweet her grief for a missing kitten one minute and praise the execution of Syrian soldiers the next? How can a young British woman write about wanting to see her prime minister's head on a spike? And always the underlying question: why, why, why would young women raised in 'freedom' choose to pledge allegiance to patriarchy in this most violent of manifestations?

The US author of *The Death of Feminism*, Phyllis Chesler, speculates that these women have chosen 'unfreedom' in response to a surfeit of choices offered to them in the West. On the *Quadrant* blog, economist Peter Smith writes that Amira Karroum's story illustrates that the 'moderate Muslims' extolled by multiculturalists are a myth.

But of course the most pervasive trope is that of the jihadi bride, the woman lured by her deviant craving for the love of a monstrous man. This focus on matrimony follows a well-established pattern in which men's motives are thought to be political while women's are assumed to be personal. However, researchers into waves of female participants in previous violent insurgencies have found that women's reasons for joining such movements were often highly political while men were not devoid of personal motivation. As much as I dislike reproducing a tweet from Umm Waqqas, an alleged jihadi recruiter (eventually revealed by Channel 4 as Rawdah Abdisalaam of Seattle) whose online messages are believed to have influenced several young women to travel to Syria to join IS, her point in the quote at the head of this chapter is worth taking seriously. While it is true that a number of the young women and girls who have travelled to Syria to join ISIS have married soon after arriving (in some cases with the match apparently arranged online in advance), it is far from clear that matrimony was their primary motivation. Given that it is not possible for lone women to live independently within the territory controlled by ISIS, the motive may in fact run in the opposite direction – they got married in order to live in the ISIS-declared caliphate, not the other way around. As Joumanah El Matrah of the Australian Muslim Women's Centre for Human Rights sees it, 'These are young women who wanted to be included in the Daesh's stated project of building a new caliphate. They've located the only entry point available to them.' Researchers have named a range of 'push' and 'pull' factors leading young women towards IS, including the experience of discrimination, grievances relating to foreign policy, and the search for independence. Pull factors include ideological motivations, the belief that IS was providing women with empowerment, and the belief that they were fulfilling a religious obligation. While some female migrants made their decision independently, others were coerced or deceived.

Certainly, the female migrants' role upon arrival was not limited to matrimony and childbirth, despite the physical limits upon them. As described by author and academic Katharina Von Knop:

The function of the women in religious terrorism organizations and movements is multifaceted. The role the world audience perceives is the one of a suicide bomber but the role of an ideological supporter and operational facilitator is not less important for the survival of the organization, the maintenance of the operational capabilities, and the ideological motivation.

Many of the women and girls posted photographs in which they posed with weapons, suggesting that they were ready to go into battle. However, Nelly Lahoud noted in 2015 that official ISIS channels do not indicate that they are open to receiving women in combat. Her previous research shows that 'jihadi ideologues have not permitted women to take part in jihad/combat, therefore limiting their role to promoting jihad by inciting their brothers, cousins etc. . . . and for sticking to traditional (mothers and wives of jihadis) or conservative ways of promoting jihad (such as writing, raising money and the like)'.

As Lahoud observes, it is difficult if not impossible for women to participate in combat operations without having to mingle with non-related males – an absolute prohibition for jihadi ideology. However, ISIS's attitude on this topic seems to have softened as it began to lose control over the territory that it had proclaimed as its caliphate, with the organisation posting articles in which it stated that armed jihad was now obligatory for women as well as men and then posting footage of a woman apparently participating in combat. Analysts, however, disagree over whether this represents a fundamental revision of ISIS's previous philosophy confining women's 'jihad' to their household, reproductive and propaganda functions. Yet it is revealing of the gendered assumptions of the counter-extremist discourse that these are uniformly designated as support roles rather than as (at least on occasion) management.

Debates Around Response

The issue of how best to respond to this issue is complicated by the fact that many of the female migrants who have travelled to the so-called Islamic State have been girls or young women who occupy the liminal zone between childhood and adulthood. Even some of those who were legally over-age when they left, or tried to leave, were still living with their parents and engaged in full-time study. They were leading dependent lives not substantially different to the lives they led as high school students. In a conversation with me in 2015, Joumanah El Matrah said:

> I think we need to consider these young women in different groups. Some are children and the system needs to work with them as children, albeit children who have aspirations towards self agency, which need to be treated respectfully. I think we should also keep in mind that the Daesh message is one that I believe is also designed and delivered by young people. Daesh is in many ways a young people's enterprise.

Sara Khan from the UK NGO Inspire (as reported by the *Guardian*) said: 'We need to stop using the phrase "jihadi brides". This is grooming, a child safety issue, and we need to make that distinction. These are normal teenage girls who should be in school, with their families, and have sacrificed everything to run off and join this crazed group.'

Khan is correct in saying that the authorities ought to treat this as a child protection issue – not an easy stance to maintain when so much of the public discussion describes them as witches to be burnt at the stake rather than children in need of care. However, in speaking to and about them, we are much more likely to strike a chord if we regard them as young adults rather than as children, bearing in mind that those urging them to join the struggle in Syria have told them that they are adult women, old enough to marry, to have children, to dedicate their lives to a greater struggle and, if necessary, to die for it.

Mixed Messages

On the one hand, parents are urged to allow their daughters the 'freedom' of life in a Western society, on the other hand to keep their offspring (sons and daughters alike) under constant surveillance for signs of radicalisation. Sara Khan urges parents to hide their daughters' passports in order to prevent them from running away. But this type of advice clashes with that provided to women and girls by many women's NGOs (often with government endorsement) about how to safely exit controlling and abusive families. Karma Nirvana, the UK-based charity that helps victims or potential victims of forced marriage, advises girls who fear they are being taken abroad to be forcibly married to hide a spoon in their underwear in order to set off airport metal detectors and attract official attention. For many young Muslim women and girls, the problem is not a lack of parental supervision, but excessive parental surveillance. Now, such surveillance has received a government mandate as being in the national interest. As suggested in *Becoming Mulan?* by Carolyn Hoyle et al.:

> Policy makers should endeavour to support families in their efforts to prevent their daughters from migrating. They should invest in interventions which advise families

on the measures, such as withholding passports and large amounts of money, that are effective in preventing their younger daughters from migrating. Furthermore, as has been shown, families have a great deal of emotional influence on their children. For this reason, counter messages coming from family members may have greater effect.

Healthy family relationships certainly play a role, but this ought not to be conflated with the securitisation of family welfare. For Joumanah El Matrah, 'This is the most disturbing development. It will not only bring surveillance into the home, but co-opt parents into the surveillance of their children, effectively making parents part of the state's security apparatus. There's nowhere now Muslim youth are not being monitored.'

Sara Khan wrote an open letter to young women who might be considering joining ISIS published in the *Guardian*, among other outlets. Opening with 'Dear Sister', she introduces herself as a fellow Muslim and cites Islamic scholars and verses from the Qur'an to tell them that ISIS's treatment of women and religious minorities is against the core principles of their religion. She closes by appealing to them to think of the grief that their disappearance and possible death would cause their mothers. This appeal may well hit home with at least some of the girls concerned – or it may miss the mark completely. Mothers – even devoted mothers – may well be one of the factors the daughters are seeking to escape. After all, they've been told that they are now old enough to become mothers themselves.

The Fate of the Cubs

Of course, the primary role of the female migrants was to provide the now-defunct caliphate with its so-called 'cubs'. The 2018 report warns that '[t]he potential for significant numbers of IS orphans and stateless minors is stark', with at least 730 children born to foreign nationals within the 'caliphate', including 566 born to western Europeans alone. These children will clearly suffer from the after-effects of trauma (trauma which for many of them is ongoing) for which they will need significant support. But, again, this is not a unique or an unprecedented occurrence. Child survivors of other war zones, including some child soldiers, have recovered sufficiently from their past to establish secure and productive post-conflict lives. But, of course, most such survivors have not carried the additional burden of being labelled as infant terrorists and monsters whose deaths can be regarded as regrettable collateral damage.

In fact, remarks by the then aspiring president Donald Trump in 2015 indicate that he would not even regard those deaths as regrettable. In 2015, Trump told his interviewers on *Fox & Friends*: 'The other thing with the terrorists is you have to take out their families. They care about their lives, don't kid yourself. When they say they don't care about their lives, you have to take out their families.'

Among those to have been 'taken out' with their families are British migrant Sally Jones, the 'former punk rocker' and ISIS recruit, who is reported to have died along with her twelve-year-old son Jojo in an airstrike in June 2017. Jojo had featured in an ISIS propaganda video which appeared to show him executing prisoners as part of a firing squad. After his death, unnamed sources were reported as having told *The Times* newspaper that, though steps would have been taken to avoid killing him, he would have been regarded as 'collateral damage' under newly introduced Trump administration guidelines that removed the stipulation that there should be a 'near certainty' of no civilian deaths before such strikes were authorised. However, even under the Obama administration, such deaths were dismissed as a regrettable necessity. After being asked about the killing of the sixteen-year-old son of the US al-Qaeda propagandist Anwar al-Awlaki in a US airstrike in Yemen in 2011, Obama campaign adviser Robert Gibbs commented that 'I would suggest that you should have a far more responsible father if they are truly concerned about the wellbeing of their children.' Al-Awlaki's eight-year-old daughter was killed along with other civilians in a January 2018 raid reportedly personally approved by Donald Trump.

Tara Nettleton, who followed her husband Khaled Sharrouf to Syria from Australia in 2014, was one of the most prominent female migrants. Nettleton and Sharrouf achieved global notoriety after Sharrouf tweeted a photograph of his seven-year-old son clutching a severed head – an image described by then-US Secretary of State John Kerry as 'one of the most disturbing, stomach-turning, grotesque photographs ever displayed'.

The graphic photograph led some Australian politicians and commentators to conclude that Sharrouf's son would have to bear responsibility for the sins of his father. Commenting on the gruesome image in an article headlined

'Australia is not their home anymore', journalist David Penberthy wrote that the Sharrouf children were too dangerous to be allowed to return to the country of their birth. 'If you've been raised by Sharrouf, you've been taught that Australia is exactly the kind of country where you should practice your despicable brand of violence. Civil society wouldn't be their sanctuary, civil society would be their target.'

Nettleton died of appendicitis in Syria, while Sharrouf was killed in a drone attack in 2017 along with two of his sons (including the child featured in the notorious photograph). His surviving children and grandchild, however, remain unaccounted for at the time of writing. His eldest daughter was married to another Australian ISIS fighter at the age of fourteen and was soon left widowed with a baby daughter. And Sharrouf's son remains the archetype of the child terrorist who must sadly be held responsible for his parents' crimes, no matter how little agency he may have had at the time.

As his obituaries noted, there was very little grief to be found for Khaled Sharrouf, who had been stripped of his Australian citizenship in 2015. And yet Sharrouf was a product of the Australian educational, criminal justice and mental health systems – a man whose diagnosed schizophrenia was left untreated for long periods of time while he was incarcerated for anti-terrorism offences, whose behaviour reportedly underwent 'a remarkable turnaround' when he received medication but who was not provided with adequate mental healthcare following his release and who was then able to use his brother's passport to slip out of the country to Syria. He is a monster of Australia's own making, who was then negligently unleashed into the world where he committed horrors against the girls whom he enslaved and raped, the men and boys whom he tortured and killed, and his own children who served as his captive audience.

Now twelve-year-old Abdullah and eleven-year old Zarqawi Sharrouf are dead. Other primary school-aged 'cubs', including offspring of British and European 'migrants', have appeared in online videos and films in which they are shown undergoing weapons training and participating in executions. These children have been 'orphaned' in more than one sense of the word, with governments and societies reluctant to claim responsibility for their future welfare. Home Affairs Minister Peter Dutton said of the Sharrouf children: 'Nobody would want to see Australian children die. Nobody would want to see any children die. But the fact is that Sharrouf and his wife took their children into a war zone. If they have been killed, what other outcome would they expect?'

But Abdullah and Zarqawi were killed in a targeted attack in which Australian intelligence agencies are reported to have played a key role, according to a report in *The Australian* newspaper. Shrugging this off as an issue of no concern is not a strong foundation for discussions with the mothers of any other 'cubs', whether they are based in the ruins of the former caliphate or within the West.

On the Home Front

Unable to make *hijra* (migrate) to the former so-called caliphate, a number of women and girls have already undertaken or allegedly attempted to undertake attacks in their countries of residence – most notably the 2015 attack by the husband and wife in San Bernardino which killed fourteen people, the three women charged with terrorism offences after a car packed with gas cylinders was found near Notre Dame Cathedral in Paris in 2016, and the mother and two daughters described as 'the first all-female ISIS terror cell' who were convicted of planning an attack on the British Museum in London in 2018.

This renewed danger on the home front means that, despite the fall of the physical caliphate in Syria and Iraq, Muslim communities remain under pressure to self-police, with women in particular on notice to play their part in 'combating violent extremism'. Politicians and police emphasise the important role played by mothers, grand-mothers and sisters in helping to prevent their male (and now increasingly female) relatives from becoming embroiled in extremist movements. Young Muslims must be watched wherever they go, online and off – and their families and community leaders must maintain constant vigilance. Community projects have been securitised to the point where a programme run by the Australian Multicultural Foundation to teach computer skills to Muslim mothers was described as an initiative to help them fight Islamic State. Similarly, in 2016 then-UK Prime Minister David Cameron announced a £20 million fund to help immigrant women learn English, focusing on the need for Muslim women to gain English language fluency as a safeguard against radicalisation. Critics highlighted the fact that that the fund was not sufficient to offset previous government cuts to language tuition, as well as pointing to the dangers of linking poor English language skills to terrorism. For David Cameron, however, inadequate English language skills combined with the 'traditional submissiveness of Muslim women' were among the driving factors leading to extremism because it left the women ill-equipped to speak out against radical imams. Muslim women responded with a series of mocking tweets using the hashtag #traditionallysubmissive in which they listed their educational, professional and personal achievements.

The shooting of police force accountant Curtis Cheng by fifteen-year-old Farhad Jabar (whose twenty-year-old sister had departed Sydney for Syria a day before the attack) in October 2015 was shocking not only because of the violence of the crime, but also the youth of the offender. The rising number of terrorism-related crimes committed by juveniles such as Jabar has intensified the scrutiny on Muslim families. Australian Foreign Minister Julie Bishop described Muslim families as 'our front line of defence against radicalized young people'. And, of course, the front line is always the most dangerous location on the battlefield.

The mood darkened still further in November 2015 after 130 people were murdered in a series of coordinated attacks around Paris that were claimed by Islamic State. A few days later, three suspected terrorists and a beloved police dog were killed during a police siege in the suburb of Saint-Denis. One of those killed was Hasna Ait Boulahcen, initially described as 'Europe's first female suicide bomber' (although Belgian woman Muriel Degauque killed herself in a suicide attack in Iraq in December 2005).

Media coverage of the attackers showed a particular fascination with Ait Boulahcen's body, including its gruesome end. She was reported to have been decapitated in the explosion that ended her life, with her head blasted out of the window and her spine landing on a police car. Analysts described how her transition from a drug-taking and promiscuous party girl to a niqab-clad extremist explained her final decision to become a 'kamikaze'. The *Daily Mail* posted a photograph of her naked in a bubble-filled bath – a photo reproduced by the *New York Post* under the headline 'Thug in a Tub'.

However, these accounts of Hasna Ait Boulahcen unravelled over subsequent days. First, police stated that she was not the bomber after all, but was killed after a man standing next to her set off his explosive device. Her body had been delivered to the hospital 'intact', not torn to shreds. And, contrary to initial reports that she had attempted to lure police to their deaths, her final words as captured on video footage ('He's not my boyfriend! Can I leave? I want to leave.') sound like a desperate plea for an exit.

And she was not the woman whose naked picture (the nipple coyly hidden by a black rectangle) was published by the *Daily Mail*. The so-called 'thug in a tub' was a Moroccan single mother whose photo was allegedly sold to the *Daily Mail* by a former friend with whom she had fallen out many years earlier. Nabila Bakkatha described herself as living in 'continuous fear' after her image was displayed around world as one of the Paris murderers.

Bakkatha was not the only one to find herself living in a climate of fear. After a Syrian passport (later reported to have been fake) was found near the body of one of the dead terrorists, reports about Europeans offering shelter and hospitality to newly arrived refugees were replaced by warnings about the security hazard that they were held to represent. In Australia, Senator Cory Bernardi said that events in Paris made him reconsider his initial support for Australia's refugee intake from Syria and Iraq and he now believed that the programme might need to be cancelled. While other cabinet ministers stated their confidence that the screening measures in place would provide sufficient protection, the initial glow of welcome had dimmed and returned to its usual mode of suspicion and paranoia.

It is important for governments and law enforcement agencies to work with rather than against Muslim families and to recognise the role played by women. However, this recognition is a double-edged sword for the women themselves as they find themselves held responsible for the actions of all concerned. Muslim women featured prominently in the meetings with community leaders undertaken by Malcolm Turnbull and NSW premier Mike Baird in the wake of the Parramatta shooting. They were castigated for this on social media by some of their fellow Muslims after the politicians alongside whom they had just been photographed announced their intention to lower the age at which suspected terrorists could be subjected to control orders from sixteen to fourteen. It is no coincidence that Muslim women's role within their families has finally been acknowledged at a time when those same families are described as pathologically dysfunctional.

Agents of Influence

The videos appearing on my Facebook feed provided some much-needed relief from the endless round of depressing events in Australia and overseas. 'Spread Hummus, Not Hate', 'Sydney Muslim Cyclists' and 'Good Luck, Usman' – the videos from the social media channel RAPT were light-hearted and often Muslim-themed. A 2017 video featured high-profile author and social advocate Yassmin Abdel-Magied talking about how to combat unconscious bias and 'hustle a job'. It was made shortly before her appearance on ABC TV's *Q&A* and the Anzac Day tweet that made her, in her own words, 'the most hated Muslim in Australia' (as discussed in chapter four). In her RAPT video, Abdel-Magied describes how unconscious bias can lead to discrimination but cheerfully tells her viewers that she is here to tell us how to 'shortcut that system, beat bias and get money'. 'Don't take it personally! Everybody has biases and just because someone is biased against you, it doesn't mean they don't like you. They just haven't gotten to know you yet.'

RAPT describes itself as 'a social news channel that explores, discovers and celebrates the stories of young Australians from mainstream and multicultural communities'. The channel is produced by a company called Breakthrough Media, which says it 'is built on successful partnerships between the Australian government, communities, civil society groups and individuals, taking a grassroots approach in assisting people to tell their stories, celebrate their achievements, and speak out against violence'.

Breakthrough Media's relationship with the British Home Office has been the subject of lengthy investigative reports in the *Guardian* and by the controversial advocacy organisation Cage. In Britain, the *Guardian*'s 2016 report noted that the Home Office used Breakthrough Media to 'promote a reconciled British Muslim identity' while keeping its involvement hidden, as 'any content or messaging attributed to the state are highly unlikely to have any credibility among these audiences'. The work was described as a series of 'clandestine propaganda campaigns'. Young Muslims were commissioned to run a government line, without ever knowing it was the government commissioning them.

As *Middle East Eye* reported, Muslim women played a key role in Breakthrough's covert communications strategy on behalf of the British government. One such project was the 'Making a Stand' campaign run by the women's counter-extremism organisation Inspire. This campaign, intended to encourage women to make a stand against terrorism, had featured on the front page of the *Sun* newspaper, with an attention-grabbing photograph of a women wearing a Union Jack hijab. And Inspire's director Sara Khan was the author of the 'Letter to my Muslim Sister', which had urged young women and girls not to support ISIS and which was now tainted by its association with clandestine government funding.

Breakthrough's Australian office had attracted little attention when I received an email from someone called Mustafa, who greeted me with 'Salam Alukum Shakira', before introducing himself as the influence manager at

214

Breakthrough Media, 'a communications agency that prides itself on telling great stories to help address complex social issues'. Breakthrough, he told me, was planning to hold a Twitter training initiative in Sydney for 'a diverse group of Australians, in particular Australian Muslims'.

This event was 'based on requests from members of the Australian Muslim community, who have advised us that a program that builds up the capacity of emerging and established leaders, especially on a platform such as Twitter, is a necessity in today's political climate'. Given my 'excellent academic background' and Twitter profile – 'I'm one of your many Twitter followers hehe' – I was regarded as a 'perfect fit' for this initiative. And, not to worry, Breakthrough would pay for my flights from Melbourne.

The invitation to Breakthrough Media's Twitter training event did not disclose any relationship with the Australian government. However, concealed in the eight-page registration survey Mustafa asked me to fill in, among the questions about dietary requirements and social media use, was a line saying the project was 'a partnership between State and Federal governments, the Australian government's Department of Home Affairs and the Office of the eSafety Commissioner'. Deep in the forms, it noted that the Countering Violent Extremism Sub-Committee, under the Australian New Zealand Counter-Terrorism Committee, 'funds this project'.

The survey asked respondents to confirm that we were prepared to meet a list of expectations for participants in the 'Voice Accelerator Workshop', including that we were willing to be active on Twitter and attend the workshop, that we were 'willing to assess opportunities, supported by Breakthrough, to participate in online discussions that align with your interests', and that we share 'the values of the project, which are: Courage, Participation, Diversity, Respect, Connection, Expression, Accuracy'. It asked that we 'respect Breakthrough's need to be politically neutral, while we respect everyone's right to express their political opinion'. Wondering whether anyone would actually self-identify as being opposed to motherhood values such as courage and respect, I ticked 'yes'.

A few weeks later, I arrived at a harbour-side conference venue in Woolloomooloo, Sydney. The thirty-odd participants were seated at designated tables of four or five as Mustafa – a young man, smartly dressed in a suit and tie – introduced himself as our MC. He told us that others in the room included Muslim and non-Muslim sportspeople, academics and people who worked in the business and tech sectors, from Perth, Adelaide, Melbourne, Canberra and Sydney – all potential positive influencers. Mustafa was 'a bit of an influencer', having built up a large Twitter following, posting about his favourite football team. He loved football, pasta, curry and sunsets on the beach. All food served on the day would of course be halal and prayer space was available.

The overall theme of the day was that 'divisive commentators' were having a negative effect on Australian society, that Muslims were bearing the brunt of this, and that it was important for voices like 'ours' to be heard. With no futher mention of the fact that the government had funded this programme, we were informed: 'We know that Muslim communities are often the most overlooked or misrepresented in the online space. Governments alone cannot redirect these narratives, but they can support those who do so.'

I recognised several familiar faces among the participants – Muslim academics, postgraduate students and community leaders. I was seated at a table with a middle-aged male Muslim academic and a young Muslim man wearing a football jersey. We had been told that we might be photographed or filmed at the workshop, and photographers and camera crews were discreetly visible in the background.

In itself, most of the content presented at the workshop would not have been contentious for most Muslims living in Australia. Aside from a session from the adviser to the Office of the eSafety Commissioner, the various presentations were led by external private providers and were probably similar to those provided to their corporate clients on media diversity, Twitter training and resilience training. Yet I was left feeling deeply concerned by the workshop and by Breakthrough's shadowy role in Australian public discourse.

Just as the disclosure about the workshop's funding had been hidden deep in the pre-workshop survey, we were also fleetingly told that 'a representative of the federal government' was attending the workshop, without being told the name of the department concerned. After directly asking Breakthrough staff for more information, I was told that the representative – Fiona Crawford of the Department of Home Affairs – would be happy to answer my questions. Crawford is a former executive producer for ABC News, a former Liberal National Party staffer in Home Affairs Minister Peter Dutton's home state of Queensland

and an unsuccessful LNP Queensland Senate candidate in the 2016 federal election. Her presence at the Voice Accelerator Workshop and her background in media made me wonder just how closely Dutton's Home Affairs department was working with Breakthrough in shaping its 'positive social impact through communications'.

Mustafa closed the day by telling us we could drop our lanyards into a bucket to signal that we were willing to accept weekly packages of information in our various areas of interest. These areas were broken down as news and current affairs, sport, arts and culture, science and technology. The idea was that we would share this weekly information on social media and help to push out positive messages. Those messages, I now understand, would be the government line for Muslims. The 1980s power anthem 'Nothing's Gonna Stop Us Now' blasted through the speakers as we were sent out into the world to make our voices heard – or, rather, to make Breakthrough's voice heard.

I chose 'news and current affairs' as the topic for my information package. The first two weeks of content were remarkably apolitical. The focus of the first package was Ramadan, with a series of tweets from Muslims around the world, followed by a package on the British royal wedding and then a notification of the pending appearance by Randa Abdel-Fattah on that week's episode of the Australian Broadcasting Corporation's talk show *Q&A* – which, we were reminded, was an important time of the week for any aspiring 'influencers' to be online. The list of likely topics for discussion did not mention the United States embassy's move to Jerusalem or the killing of Palestinian protesters in Gaza – events that had taken place that week and which loomed large in the consciousness of Muslims around the world. And, in fact, the *Q&A* debate featured heated disagreement on this topic between Abdel-Fattah and journalist Greg Sheridan.

The workshop participants were repeatedly assured that our participation was voluntary, that we could withdraw at any point, and that we were under no obligation to share material unless we thought it was worth endorsing. These reassurances seemed odd. It would not have occurred to me that I was under any obligation to share content from an organisation that was not employing me and with whom I had never had any contractual relationship.

Of course, sharing this content is the point. As in Britain, Peter Dutton's department was hoping to shape a unified voice for Good Muslims. This unified voice is propaganda.

I realised while researching Breakthrough that several videos and memes from RAPT had appeared in my Facebook feed after being shared by friends who were unaware of any connection to the Home Affairs Department. The content is light-hearted and feel-good and does not have any obvious political agenda. And yet in deflecting attention away from critical voices and towards a supposed consensus of contentment, it serves a clear propaganda purpose. 'They're securitizing *happiness!*' I complained to a friend, after viewing one of these friendly, cheerful videos.

After attending the Voice Accelerator Workshop, I emailed Yassmin Abdel-Magied to ask her about her experience making the video for RAPT. She confirmed that Breakthrough approached her to produce the video but did not disclose its relationship with government.

'They initially emailed and as they'd been given my name through someone I knew, I thought there was no harm in getting involved,' she told me:

> I didn't know that they were funded by government at all actually – they simply said they were 'a social news channel that celebrates the diversity of the next generations of Australians and has a particular focus on strengthening the ties between Muslim and non-Muslim Australians'.
>
> I was intrigued, but didn't ask too many questions … They seemed nice, a bit vague about how they'd started or who they were, but seemed to have good intentions, which gave me some level of comfort. I don't recall someone from government being there – at least, there was no one introduced like that.

After publishing an article about Breakthrough Media for the *Saturday Paper*, I was contacted by a number of female friends who described similar approaches to that received by Abdel-Magied – people who introduced themselves via friends or family members before suggesting that they work with them on a creative project. Once again, Breakthrough had not disclosed their relationship with government. Those who had been made unwitting mouthpieces for a government department whose agenda they deeply distrusted expressed a sense of shock. Father Rod Bowers of the Anglican Parish of Gosford, whose church signs regularly make headlines for their support for refugees and denunciations of racism, had participated in a RAPT video about the signs. He tweeted my article about Breakthrough with the comment: 'I was used by Breakthrough Media too. Now I feel dirty.'

For its part, the Home Affairs department responded to the article with a short statement on its website in which it confirmed that it had a contract with Breakthrough Media and that the workshop I had attended had been held as part of that contract. The statement also said that 'the Australian government was a known sponsor of the event' and that 'the Department does not undertake covert unattributable communication activity'. And it is true that participants at the workshop were technically informed about the department's funding – but only if we had bothered to read the fine print of an eight-page survey.

The Australian government had previously addressed the suspicion surrounding its CVE-related 'Living Safe Together' grants by not disclosing the names of some of the organisations to receive funding under the scheme. However, this lack of disclosure only spreads the net of suspicion more widely so that anyone 'speaking out against extremism' – not a particularly marginal view among Muslims living in Australia – risks sounding like a government mouthpiece. This is particularly the case for Muslim women, given the government's securitised representation of issues around Islam and gender.

To use an old Cold War term, then, Muslim women living in the West are now all potential 'agents of influence' for one side or the other as the War on Terror enters the realm of domestic politics in its most intimate sense. How are we to know who to trust, when we ourselves may have been unknowingly recruited by someone else's propaganda war?

CONCLUSION

In the years since September 2001, Muslim women have become far more visible participants in Western public life in fields ranging from entertainment to media and politics. Yet this mainstream success has done little to slow the routine harassment of visibly Muslim women in public space, the opportunist deployment of 'the Muslim problem' as a diversionary tactic by mainstream politicians, or the rise of far-right parties who have made the need to protect Western women and girls against the encroachment of Muslim gender norms a central element of their *raison d'être*. Muslim women are no longer required to simply stand in veiled silence, waiting to be rescued. Rather, they should follow the advice of politicians such as Boris Johnson and remove their 'ridiculous' veils of their own accord, lest they be mistaken for letter boxes or bank robbers.

If Muslim women found themselves locked in a fraught double-bind in their roles as victims, the dilemma confronting them in their roles as suspects is no less hazardous. The increased securitisation of all elements of Muslim public and private life has made it all but impossible for Muslim women to undertake productive conversations among ourselves on vital topics such as gendered violence, reproductive rights, social and economic marginalisation, and the rising threat of far-right as well as Muslim extremism. These issues now confront not only those Muslim women who were born or have long been settled in the West, but the cohort of new migrants who have travelled from the various post-9/11 war zones, only to find themselves singled out as objects of intense suspicion.

No More Muslim Men

In September 2015, Europe faced what was described as its worst refugee crisis since the Second World War as an influx of asylum-seekers from the conflicts in Syria and Iraq joined those fleeing war-zones in locations ranging from Afghanistan to sub-Saharan Africa. According to the United Nations High Commission for Refugees (UNHCR), more than 300,000 refugees made the sea-crossing from Turkey to Greece and Italy in the first eight months of the year, compared to 219,000 during the whole of 2014. The death toll also rose steeply, with 3,000 people estimated to have died or gone missing trying to reach Europe during 2014, while an estimated 2,500 met a similar fate during the first eight months of 2015.

Steve McCurry's 'Afghan Girl' photograph had symbolised a previous generation of refugees. Now the image of another young child came to represent the new global refugee crisis. But, while Sharbat Gula had been fiercely, definitely alive as she looked into the lens of the camera, the photograph of three-year-old Aylan (Alan) Kurdi showed his lifeless body face down on a Turkish beach after the dinghy transporting his family and fourteen other asylum-seekers to Greece sank in heavy seas.

The photograph of Aylan Kurdi provoked a global wave of sympathy towards the refugees who were risking their lives crossing the Mediterranean in search of safety. Donations to the Red Cross appeal to aid Syrian refugees spiked and vigils held in his memory around the world called upon governments to open their borders to those seeking aslyum. Two days after his death, Germany agreed to admit the thousands of refugees that had been stranded in Hungary, while David Cameron announced that the United Kingdom would admit 4,000 refugees a year until 2020. The governments of the European Union eventually reached an agreement to 'burden-share' the resettlement of 120,000 members of the refugee influx.

However, the empathy that was extended towards Aylan Kurdi apparently did not apply to the adult males who were attempting to undertake the journey that had claimed his life. Then presidential candidate Donald Trump told Fox News that he was concerned at 'how many of the people in the migration were strong young men. You look at them. I'm saying, Where are the women? Where are the children? We're taking in people we have no idea who they are.' The refugee intake, he continued, 'could turn out to be the greatest Trojan horse of all time'.

Trump was not alone in noticing the disproportionate number of men – and strong young men at that – in the footage of refugees who had travelled to Europe in 2015. But, then, given the dangerous nature of the journey, it's hardly surprising that the physically strongest members of the family would go on ahead in the hope of finding safer exit routes for others once they reached their destination. Although 62 per cent of the migrants to have travelled to Europe in 2015 were men, the gender profile among those registered with the UNHCR in Egypt, Iraq, Jordan and Lebanon was more or less evenly split.

Soon-to-be-deposed Australian Prime Minister Tony Abbott initially refused to increase the nation's refugee intake to help accommodate those displaced by the escalation of conflict in the Middle East. However, on this as with many other issues, he had misjudged the national mood. As large vigils were held around the nation to commemorate Aylan Kurdi, conservative columnists as well as senior members of Abbott's own party were among those to call for Australia to admit more Syrian refugees. Faced with this broad-based appeal, Abbott eventually announced that an extra 12,000 places would be provided for refugees from Syria and Iraq.

But there would be telling criteria for the extra resettlement places. As Abbott emphasised, the intake would focus on 'women, children and families of persecuted minorities'. Under questioning, he added that the intake would also include some members of persecuted Muslim minorities, thus dodging allegations that the scheme excluded Muslims alto-gether. However, during the lead-up to Abbott's announce-ment, ABC journalists Anna Henderson and Chris Uhlmann reported that 'the message being sent to the Prime Minister by some in the Coalition was "No more Muslim men"'.

Prior to becoming prime minister, Abbott's successor Malcolm Turnbull had been among those who expressed support for focusing on Christians in the Syrian refugee intake, telling journalists that post-war Syria was unlikely to provide a space for its 'ancient' Christian communities. Once in office, he and Foreign Minister Julie Bishop reiterated that the refugee intake would focus on members of those commu-nities such as Christians and Yazidis who faced an 'existential threat' and would never be able to return to the region even after the end of the war. Nor did Turnbull take any measures to modify the policy of excluding single men from the intake, despite the fact that purportedly gay men have featured in some of the most brutal of ISIS's notorious snuff movies.

Canada provided a feel-good story at the height of the refugee crisis, with footage of Justin Trudeau personally welcoming Syrian refugees to Canada at the airport and greeting them with the words, 'You are home.' But, in November 2015, Trudeau followed Turnbull's lead by announcing that Canada's refugee intake would prioritise families and religious minorities; unlike Turnbull, however, he included LGBT individuals on the list of priorities. Applications from single, straight men, he told the media, were 'slightly more complicated' and would need to be deferred or denied because 'there will be a few people who will be surprisingly problematic'.

No more Muslim men, in other words.

At first glance, a policy that prioritises women and children ahead of unmarried men may seem equal parts chivalrous and feminist. After all, women and girls face high levels of gender-based violence – sexual violence in particular – on top of the many other hazards of refugee life. However, a policy which is exclusionary rather than needs based is an inadequate means of addressing this. Women themselves seldom conceptualise their welfare in such limited terms. I was taken by surprise by how prominently the welfare of men and boys featured in the concerns of the Afghan women I interviewed in refugee camps in Pakistan such as the girl described in Chapter 1 who listed the hardships faced by her brothers as her main source of grief. She and her sisters spent most of their time at home with their mother, just as they had done in Afghanistan. Her brothers, on the other hand, were forced to engage in dangerous and backbreaking labour in the brick kilns, rather than working their family's own land as they had done before their displacement. Nor does a policy that so heavily emphasises women's inability to fend for themselves after displacement do justice to women's ability to adapt and to acquire new skills in order to support themselves and their families.

Protecting the most vulnerable, then, is also a useful way of excluding the post 9/11 folk-devil – the Muslim male. Women are admitted on the basis that they are helpless and docile, and they carry the expectation that they will exert a civilising influence on any men and boys who may accompany them.

In January 2016, the French satirical magazine *Charlie Hebdo* published a cartoon titled 'Migrants'. The cartoon featured the famous image of Kurdi's body lying on the beach alongside the question 'Que serait devenu le petit Aylan s'il avait grandi?' ('What would little Aylan have grown up to be?') The answer is illustrated as a couple of leering adult males chasing a scantily dressed woman through the streets with the words, 'Tripoteur de fesses en Allemagne' ('an arse-groper in Germany'). While some commentators described the cartoon as a misguided attempt to satirise racism rather than to depict children such as Aylan as sexual predators in the making, the *Washington Post* noted, 'In hindsight, the death of Aylan Kurdi . . . may mark the high point in European public support for refugees.'

The event referenced by the *Charlie Hebdo* cartoon was the episode in which hundreds of women attending New Year celebrations in Cologne reported having been sexually assaulted and robbed by 'north African-looking men'. The offenders were widely assumed to be asylum-seekers, despite the lack of information about their identities.

The so-called 'Cologne terror' not only dimmed the glow of the *Willkommenskultur* in Germany, but also fuelled anti-refugee sentiment around the globe. Then presidential candidate Donald Trump tweeted: 'Germany is going through massive attacks to its people by the migrants allowed to enter the country. New Year's Eve was a disaster. THINK!' Fear of an unregulated influx of refugees from elsewhere in the European Union helped to fuel the 'Leave' vote in the Brexit referendum in June 2016, with UKIP leader Nigel Farage claiming that a 'Remain' victory would place British women at risk of similar attacks to those inflicted upon the women in Cologne. In Germany itself, anti-refugee incidents included attacks on refugee housing as well as male refugees being refused entry to a swimming pool on the ground that they might harass female swimmers.

The story of the Cologne assaults resonated with incidents including the Rochdale grooming gangs in the United Kingdom, in which a network of mostly Asian men had preyed upon vulnerable young girls, and a 2016 gang rape in a predominantly Muslim suburb of Stockholm, which sparked demonstrations around the nation after five male immigrants were eventually found not guilty. For Australians, this trope of the Muslim immigrant as sexual predator revived memories of the so-called 'Sydney gang-rapes' – a series of assaults by mostly Muslim men which took place in 2000 but which came to trial in the years immediately following 9/11.

Racialised reporting of sexual assaults has arguably contributed as much as terrorism in establishing the figure of the young Muslim male as folk-devil. The spectre of the Muslim sexual predator has become well enough established to have made at least two high-profile fictional appearances. In the first case, in Sydney, senior journalist Paul Sheehan (who had written a book about the Sydney gang rape trials) wrote a report for the *Sydney Morning Herald* about a woman whom he called 'Louise', who claimed to have been gang-raped and seriously injured by a group of men she said were known as 'MERCs' (or 'Middle Eastern Raping Cunts'). However, after police and hospital records were unable to substantiate her claim and videos emerged of 'Louise' addressing a Reclaim Australia rally, the newspaper retracted the story and Sheehan was placed on leave, never to return. In the second case, the German newspaper *Bild* published claims by a bar owner in Frankfurt about a 'Muslim sex mob' who had invaded his bar, robbing customers and sexually assaulting women, one of whom provided an account of her traumatic experience. However, the lack of witnesses and the fact that the alleged victim had not been in the country on the night in question forced the newspaper to apologise and retract the story. The bar owner and the 'victim' were awaiting trial for falsely reporting a crime when he was arrested for her murder, apparently over a financial dispute.

Even though Muslim men and boys are the primary focus of these moral panics, they also have a significant impact on Muslim women and girls. Aside from the stigma attached to their families and communities, they themselves are regarded as occupying a privileged status in comparison to their non-Muslim counterparts when it comes to this particular type of crime. It has been well established over many years that most sexual violence takes place within tribal boundaries, not across them, yet Muslim women are popularly assumed to be immune from attacks by Muslim sexual offenders. And, just as Muslim mothers are rendered suspect for their supposed role in raising potential terrorists, they are also held responsible for raising their sons to regard non-Muslim women and girls as legitimate prey.

The far-right demand to 'Stop the rapefugees' echoed well beyond Europe's shores. It was the slogan of choice at a small far-right rally in the Melbourne suburb of Eltham in which I observed speakers proclaim the need to 'protect our women' from asylum-seekers who had 'committed rape and pillage across Europe'. The rally took place a few days before the 2016 presidential election, and one of the young women at the rally was wearing a Donald Trump T-shirt – the first piece of Trump merchandise that I had set eyes on. At the time, the 'pussygate' footage seemed to have put paid to Trump's candidacy. A Clinton presidency and a continuation of the imperial feminist mission to rescue Muslim women seemed assured.

Of course, this was not to be. Trump's victory flicked the switch towards the disciplining of Muslim women, men and children alike as his executive order imposed his promised immigration ban in the form of an absolute veto on entry for travellers and migrants from six Muslim-majority nations and a severely curtailed refugee intake. But, even as Australians were shocked by the chaotic scenes at airports across the United States as the executive order took hold, some pointed out that they were in no position to consider themselves morally superior. This was a point made by Trump himself in a phone conversation with Prime Minister Malcolm Turnbull in which Turnbull tried to convince Trump to deliver on Obama's promise to resettle refugees from Australia's offshore detention camps. As Turnbull notes, these refugees had been in detention for three years by this time.

In the transcript of the phone call leaked to the *Washington Post*, Turnbull explains to Trump that he is not trying to offload the refugees to him because they were considered unworthy candidates, but because of Australia's absolute prohibition on admitting those who had attempted to enter the country by boat. 'So we said if you try to come to the country by boat, even if we think you're the best person in the world, even if you're a Noble [sic] prize-winning genius, we will not let you in.'

Trump responded approvingly: 'That is a good idea. We should do that too. You're worse than I am.'

The arrival of 'mainly Muslim asylum-seekers' (as they were referred to in media reports) by boat had been a prominent feature of Australian public discourse throughout the post 9/11 era, thanks to the August 2001 Tampa affair. Prime Minister John Howard's uncompromising declaration that 'We will decide who comes to this country and the circumstances in which they come' was widely regarded as a decisive factor in his party's election victory in November 2001. In the years since then, both sides of politics have imposed a series of ever-more punitive measures to 'stop the boats', with boat arrivals initially held in remote detention centres in Australia and then later in offshore detention centres on Manus Island in Papua New Guinea and in Nauru. This culminated in the legislation introduced in 2016 under the government of Kevin Rudd which ruled that those who attempted to get to Australia by boat would never be granted a visa to enter the country. Those already held on Manus Island and Nauru could either return home or seek resettlement in a third country.

In 2017, as European governments sought to manage their own influx of boat arrivals, both Australian Prime Minister Malcolm Turnbull and his predecessor Tony Abbott gave public lectures in Europe (Abbott in London and Turnbull in Germany) in which they described the success of Australia's hard-line policy in halting the flow of unregulated asylum-seekers. And, as Sasha Polakow-Suransky reported for the *Guardian*, the 'Australian solution' – boat-turnbacks and offshore detention – has become popular with the leaders of Europe's far-right parties, from Nigel Farage in the United Kingdom to Yohann Faviere from France's Front National to Frits Bolkestein from the Netherlands' centre-right VVD party to Italy's deputy prime minister Matteo Salvini.

As analysts such as Daniel Ghazelbash have pointed out, the measures undertaken by the Australian government were only economically feasible in dealing with the small numbers of refugees who had managed to reach Australian shores. And that is to say nothing of the human rights violations inflicted on Manus Island and Nauru, with female refugees particularly vulnerable to abuses, including 'groping, touching, explicit threats, and rape'. In his 2018 report on 'Australia's refugee gulag' for *Foreign Policy*, Mark Isaacs describes cases including a six-year-old girl who had tried to hang herself with a fence tie and another girl 'not yet a teenager' whom an Australian judge had ordered to be transferred from Nauru to a psychiatric facility in Australia because not to do so would leave her at high risk of suicide. As Isaacs notes, Home Affairs Minister Peter Dutton has resisted allowing such transfers on the grounds that some refugees were 'self-harming and people have self-immolated in order to get to Australia'.

Faced with these kinds of reports, it is difficult to disagree with Trump's evaluation of Australia as worse than the United States in its treatment of irregular (mostly Muslim) migrants – men, women and children alike.

Social Media as a Double-Edged Sword

Social media may not carry the physical dangers of war zones and detention centres, but it has nonetheless often been a hostile environment for Muslim women. For example, in the wake of the Westminster attack in 2017, a post showing a photograph of a woman in hijab checking her phone while walking past an injured victim went viral. The photo was captioned 'Muslim woman pays no mind to the terror attack, casually walks past a dying man while checking her phone', with the hashtags #PrayforLondon and #BanIslam. The photographer spoke out in defence of the woman concerned, sharing a second photograph in which her distress was more apparent, and the account that had created the post was later revealed to have been a Russian bot. But, by the time these corrections were issued, the damage had already been done.

This tense situation has not deterred Muslim women from finding creative ways to speak out and to connect with their co-religionists around the globe. In February 2018, Pakistani woman Sabica Khan shared a Facebook post in which she described being sexually assaulted by men in the crowd as she performed *tawaf* at Mecca. 'My entire experience of the holy city is overshadowed by this horrible incident.' Other women offered similar testimony after journalist Mona Eltahawy posted an article that she had written on the topic with the suggestion that women share their stories using the hashtag #mosquemetoo.

And Iranian women took to social media under the hashtag #TheGirlsofRevolutionStreet, after a young woman called Vida Movahed posted a photograph on Instagram which showed her with her hair uncovered, waving her headscarf around on a stick. Movahed and thirty other young women who followed her example were promptly arrested for this violation of the country's strict dress regulations, although most were released shortly afterwards.

As Azadeh Moaveni reported for the *New Yorker*, #TheGirlsofRevolutionStreet were promptly conscripted by United States Secretary of State Mike Pompeo for the purposes of regime change in Iran. Like Lord Cromer, the nineteenth-century British consul-general of Egypt, and President George W. Bush before him, Pompeo's enthusiasm for Muslim women's rights did not reflect a feminist outlook when it came to the rights of women closer to home, serving as he did under a president who had boasted about the sexual assault of women and given his own opposition to abortion in all circumstances. This of course raised the stakes for the protesting women themselves, who were no longer simply campaigners for gender reform in their own country, but instruments of US foreign policy. Like the members of the Revolutionary Association of the Women of Afghanistan before them, they are discovering that powerful men can always find a way to weaponise women's rights.

Déjà Vu All Over Again

Some tropes from the immediate aftermath of 11 September 2001 now seem to be reappearing as a form of alt-right pantomime. In October 2001, Democrat representative Carolyn Maloney wore a burqa to the House of Representatives in order to illustrate her point about the garment's restrictive nature while delivering a speech about Taliban abuse. 'The veil is so thick it is difficult to breathe. The mesh opening for the eyes makes it extremely difficult to even cross the road.'

In August 2017, on the other hand, the Australian far-right senator Pauline Hanson entered the Senate chamber wearing a black burqa (which she later said had been purchased on e-bay) in order to demonstrate its potential use in undertaking a terrorist attack. Where Maloney had emphasised the physical limitations that the garment imposed upon the women forced to wear it, Hanson claimed that her ability to wear a burqa into the nation's parliament illustrated its usefulness for potential suicide bombers. 'No-one should be permitted behind a veil of secrecy while there is a security concern.'

Maloney's soft Taliban-blue burqa suited her narrative about oppressed and helpless Afghan women. Hanson's black burqa, on the other hand, looked altogether more menacing and sinister. Her stunt horrified her parliamentary colleagues, reducing veteran Attorney-General George Brandis almost to tears in his response.

But, given that Brandis apparently endorsed the internment of refugee men, women and children in offshore detention centres, it is difficult to believe that his tears were shed because of the harm that Hanson's stunt inflicted upon the Muslim women of Australia. Rather, as he stated, he was concerned about the damage it had done to the intelligence-gathering capabilities of the security agencies who relied on good relationships with the Muslim community. Though Brandis was careful to note that most Muslims were decent, law-abiding citizens, he could not defend them from vilification without noting the need to treat them as potential informants against the small number of suspects.

Two weeks after the attacks in Paris, I attended an anti-Muslim rally held by the far-right Reclaim Australia movement on the outskirts of Melbourne. Of course, it is important not to overstate the degree of support among non-Muslims for fringe movements such as Reclaim Australia and the English Defence League, just as it is important not to inflate the degree of support among Muslims for al-Qaeda and ISIS. However, listening to the speeches and reading the placards at the rally, I was struck by how closely their language mirrored the commonplace anti-Muslim racism that politicians and media outlets espouse every day.

As always, Muslims as a supposed threat to gender equality featured high on the list of concerns. And, of course, face-veiling was held to represent a particularly dangerous risk to national security. Like a grotesque parody of those long-ago feminist events at which women were invited try on a burqa in order to experience Taliban oppression for themselves, many of the protestors at the rally concealed their faces with either hockey masks or Australian flag bandanas.

I asked a trio of bandana-clad protestors whether they thought that Muslim face-veils should be banned. 'That's the point we're making. Do they find this intimidating? Of course they do. So we get asked to take ours off. They don't.'

And the mission to 'intimidate' rather than rescue Muslim women is not restricted to extremist organisations such as Reclaim Australia. Muslim women are told by Muslim and Western powerbrokers alike that they must determine what part they will play in the ongoing drama that is the War on Terror, and tailor their performance (and of course their costume) according to the requirements of the role.

After all, there is nothing more suspicious than a Muslim woman who insists upon writing her own lines.

REFERENCES

Introduction

Abu-Lughod, Lila, *Do Muslim Women Need Saving?*, Harvard University Press, Cambridge, MA, 2013, pp. 30–1.

Costa, Robert and Philip Rucker, 'It's a Hard Problem: Inside Trump's Decision to Send More Troops to Afghanistan', *Washington Post*, 21 August 2017.

Eltahawy, Mona, *Headscarves and Hymens*, Farrer, Straus and Giroux, New York, 2015.

Farris, Sara R., *In the Name of Women's Rights: The Rise of Femonationalism*, Duke University Press, Durham, NC, and London, 2017.

Follain, John and Rita Cristofari, *Zola's Story: An Afghan Woman's Struggle for Freedom*, William Morrow & Co., Scranton, PA, 2002.

Gallagher, Dorothy, 'Fanny Girls', *New Statesman*, vol. 130, no. 4589, 28 May 2001.

Huntington, Samuel, 'The Clash of Civilizations', lecture delivered at the American Enterprise Institute for Public Policy Research, Washington DC, 1992.

Kandiyoti, Deniz, 'Bargaining with Patriarchy', *Gender & Society*, vol. 2, no. 3, September 1988, pp. 274–90.

Lazreg, Marnia, *The Eloquence of Silence: Algerian Women in Question*, Routledge, New York, 1994.

Mohanty, Chandra Talpade, 'Under Western Eyes: Feminist Scholarship and Colonial Discourses', *Boundary 2*, vol. 12/13, issue 3, spring/autumn 1984.

Sirin, Selcuk R. and Michelle Fine, *Muslim American Youth: Understanding Hyphenated Identities through Multiple Methods*, New York University Press, New York and London, 2008.

REFERENCES

Spivak, Gayatri, *Can the Subaltern Speak?*, Columbia University Press, New York, 1988.

Tesfaye, Sophia, 'Trump defends the burqa – in the most sexist way possible: "You don't have to put on make-up"', *Salon*, 26 October 2015.

1 Afghan Girls

Abu-Lughod, Lila, *Do Muslim Women Need Saving?*, Harvard University Press, Cambridge, MA, 2013, pp. 30–1.

Antonowicz, Anton, 'Zarmina's Story', *Mirror*, 20 June 2002.

Azami, Dawood, '"Afghan Girl" Sharbat Gula in Quest for New Life', BBC News, 16 January 2017, https://www.bbc.com/news/world-asia-38640487

Brodsky, Anne, *With All Our Strength: The Revolutionary Association of the Women of Afghanistan*, Routledge, New York, 2004.

Brown, Janelle, 'The Taliban's Bravest Opponents', *Salon*, 3 October 2001.

Brzezinski, Zbigniew, interview with *Le Nouvel Observateur*, trans. William Blum and David N. Gibbs, https://dgibbs.faculty.arizona.edu/brzezinski_interview

Charania, Moon, *Will the Real Pakistani Woman Please Stand Up? Empire, Visual Culture and the Brown Female Body*, McFarland & Company Inc., Jefferson, NC, 2015.

Emadi, Hafizullah, *Repression, Resistance and Women in Afghanistan*, Greenwood Publishing Group, Santa Barbara, 2002.

Ensler, Eve, *The Vagina Monologues*, Virago, London, 2001.

Hirschkind, C. and S. Mahmood, 'Feminism, the Taliban and Politics of Counter-Insurgency', *Anthropological Quarterly*, vol. 75, no. 2, spring 2002, George Washington University Institute for Ethnographic Research.

Human Rights Watch, 'Pakistan Coercion, UN Complicity: The Mass Forced Returns of Afghan Refugees', 13 February 2017.

Jones, Ann, 'Afghan Women Have Already Been Abandoned', *The Nation*, 12 April 2010.

Khan, Shahnaz, 'The Two Faces of Afghan Women: Oppressed and Exotic', *Women's Studies International Forum*, vol. 44, May–June 2014, pp. 101–8.

Leno, Mavis, speech to launch Feminist Majority's 'Stop Gender Apartheid in Afghanistan', 1997.

Morgan, Dan and David B. Ottaway, 'Women's Fury Toward Taliban Stalls Pipeline', *Washington Post*, 11 January 1998.

Ravitz, Jessica, 'Saving Aesha', *CNN Digital Magazine*, 19 May 2012.

Stengel, Richard, 'The Plight of Afghan Women: A Disturbing Picture', *Time*, 29 July 2010, http://content.time.com/time/magazine/article/0,9171,2007415,00.html

WikiLeaks, 'CIA Report into Shoring Up Afghan War Support in Western Europe'.

2 Candle in the Wind

Ahmed, Khaled, 'Saint Qazi', *Newsweek*, 18 January 2013, http://newsweek-pakistan.com/saint-qazi/

REFERENCES

Anon. (Yousafzai, Malala), 'Diary of a Pakistani Schoolgirl', BBC, January 2009, http://news.bbc.co.uk/1/hi/world/south_asia/7834402.stm

Ashraf, Irfan, 'Malala: The Journalistic Ethics of Source Well-Being', *ViewsWeek*, 14 April 2014, www.viewsweek.com/viewsweek-exclusive/malala-the-journalistic-ethics-of-source-well-being

Brohi, Nazish and Saba Gul Khattak, 'Exploring Women's Voices', *Women's Regional Network*, Pakistan, 2008.

Cavallaro, James, Stephen Sonnenberg and Sarah Knuckey, *Living Under Drones: Death, Injury and Trauma to Civilians from US Drone Practices in Pakistan*, International Human Rights and Conflict Resolution Clinic, Stanford Law School, New York, 2012, https://law.stanford.edu/publications/living-under-drones-death-injury-and-trauma-to-civilians-from-us-drone-practices-in-pakistan/

Hussein, Shakira, 'Akbar vs the Drones: The Pakistani Lawyer Taking the US to Court', *Crikey*, 1 August 2013.

Jamal, Amina, *Jamaat-e-Islami Women in Pakistan: Vanguard of a New Modernity?*, Syracuse University Press, New York, 2013.

Khoja-Moolji, Shenila, *Forging the Ideal Educated Girl*, University of California Press, Oakland, 2018.

Khoja-Moolji, Shenila, 'Why is Malala Such a Polarising Figure in Pakistan?", Al Jazeera, 1 April 2018, https://www.aljazeera.com/indepth/opinion/malala-polarising-figure-pakistan-180401054631496.html

Krook, Mona L., *Quotas for Women in Politics: Gender and Candidate Selection Reform Worldwide*, Oxford University Press, New York, 2010.

'Malala Attack Being Used as a Cover for Waziristan Operation', *Pakistan Today*, 14 October 2012, https://www.pakistantoday.com.pk/2012/10/14/malalas-attack-being-used-as-a-cover-for-waziristan-operation/

Maududi, S.A.A. and Al-Ash'ari, 'Purdah and the Status of Women in Islam', *Islamic Publications*, Lahore, 2002.

Murtaza, Syed M., 'Why are Pakistanis Upset at Malala Getting into Oxford?', *Pakistan Today*, 18 August 2017, https://www.pakistantoday.com.pk/2017/08/18/why-are-pakistanis-upset-at-malala-getting-into-oxford/

Pew Research Center, 'Pakistani Public Opinion Ever More Critical of U.S.', Washington DC, 27 June 2012.

Shehzad, M., 'MMA Tries to Reinvent Itself', *Friday Times*, 1 November 2002.

Sherazi, Zahid Shah, 'Taliban Uses Islamic Shariah to Defend Malala Attack', *Dawn*, 12 October 2012.

Wizarat, Shahida, 'Why Was Malala Yousafzai Attacked?', *Frontier Post*, 14 October 2012.

Yiannopoulos, Milo, 'Sorry to Be Rude, But Malala Yousafzai is Becoming a Bit of a Bore', *Breitbart News*, 13 October 2014, https://www.breitbart.com/london/2014/10/13/sorry-to-be-rude-but-little-malala-yousafzai-is-becoming-a-bit-of-a-bore/

Yousafzai, Malala and Christina Lamb, *I Am Malala*, Weidenfeld & Nicolson, London, 2013.

Zia, Afiya Shehrbano, 'Being Malala', *openDemocracy*, 13 October 2009, www.opendemocracy.net/5050/afiya-shehrbano-zia/being-malala

3 Shifting Perceptions

Abu-Lughod, Lila, *Do Muslim Women Need Saving?*, Harvard University Press, Cambridge, MA, 2013.

Ahmed, Leila, *A Quiet Revolution: The Veil's Resurgence, from the Middle East to America*, Yale University Press, New Haven and London, 2011.

Ahmed, Nilofar, 'So Few Muslim Women Wear the Burqa in Europe That Banning It is a Waste of Time', *The Conversation*, https://theconversation.com/so-few-muslim-women-wear-the-burqa-in-europe-that-banning-it-is-a-waste-of-time-82957 30 August 2017

Amin, Qasim, *The Liberation of Women and The New Woman: Two Documents in the History of Egyptian Feminism*, American University in Cairo Press, Cairo, 2000.

Asad, Talal, 'French Secularism and the "Islamic Veil Affair"', *Hedgehog Review*, spring/summer, Institute for Advanced Studies in Culture, University of Virginia, 2006.

Aziz, Sahar F., 'From the Oppressed to the Terrorist: Muslim American Women Caught in the Crosshairs of Intersectionality', *Hastings Race & Poverty Law Journal*, vol. 9, no. 1, Texas A&M School of Law, Fort Worth, 2012.

Bishop, Bronwyn, 'Bronwyn Bishop calls for hijab ban in schools', interview on *The World Today*, Radio National, 29 August 2005.

Budd, Henry and Steven Deeks, 'Sydney Artist Rips the Lid Off Controversial Cover-up', *Daily Telegraph*, 24 September 2010.

El Matrah, Joumanah, 'Stolen Voices of Muslim Women', *The Age*, 22 April 2005.

Fanon, Frantz, 'Algeria Unveiled', in *A Dying Colonialism*, trans. Haakon Chevalier, Grove Press, New York, 1965.

Flynn, Eugenia, 'The Only Way to Defeat January 26 is to Come Together", NITV, 23 January 2017, https://www.sbs.com.au/nitv/article/2017/01/23/comment-only-way-defeat-january-26-come-together

Gander, Kashmira, 'Modest Fashion: How Covering Up Became Mainstream', *Independent*, 16 October 2017, https://www.independent.co.uk/life-style/fashion/modesty-fashion-shopping-covering-up-hijab-abaya-muslim-jewish-orthodox-christian-a8003726.html

Halsband, Robert (ed.), *Complete Letters of Lady Mary Wortley Montagu*, Clarendon Press, Oxford, 1965–76.

Haussegger, Virginia, 'Ban unAustralian burka', *Canberra Times*, 27 June 2009.

Helmore, Edward, 'Munira Ahmed: The Woman Who Became the Face of the Trump Resistance', *Guardian*, 23 January 2017, https://www.theguardian.com/us-news/2017/jan/23/womens-march-poster-munira-ahmed-shepard-fairey-interview

Human Rights and Equal Opportunity Commission Report, 2004.

Hussein, Shakira, 'An Evening with Yvonne Ridley, "Firebrand Radical Convert"', *Crikey*, 26 September 2014.

Hussein, S., S. Bloul and S. Poynting, 'Diasporas and Dystopias on the Beach: Burqini Wars in France and Australia', in I. Zempi and I. Awan (eds), *The Routledge Handbook: Key Readings in Islamophobia*, Routledge, London, forthcoming 2019.

Janmohamed, Shelina, *Generation M: Young Muslims Changing the World*, I.B. Tauris, London, 2016.

Kahf, Mohja, 'Packaging Huda Sha'rawi's Memoirs in the US Reading Environment', in Amal Amireh and Lisa Suhair Majaj (eds), *Going Global: The Transnational Reception of Third World Women*, Garland, New York, 2000, pp. 148–72.

Kingdon, Victoria, 'M&S launches first "burkini"', *Harper's Bazaar*, 1 April 2016.

Kurti, Peter, 'Modest Bid for Muslim Trade', Centre for Independent Studies, 8 February 2018, http://www.cis.org.au/commentary/articles/pk-article/

Mahmood, Saba, *Politics of Piety: The Islamic Revival and the Feminist Subject*, Princeton University Press, Princeton, NJ, 2004.

Malik, N., 'The Sun's "United Against ISIS" Campaign is a Proxy for Anti-Muslim Bigotry', *Guardian*, 8 October 2014, https://www.theguardian.com/commentisfree/2014/oct/08/sun-unite-against-isis-muslim-bigotry

Murphy, Damien, 'Thugs Ruled the Streets, and the Mob Sang Waltzing Matilda', *Sydney Morning Herald*, 12 December 2005.

Murphy, Katharine, 'Burqa Theft Prompts Abbott to Echo Howard's Concerns', *The Age*, 7 May 2010.

Obama, Barack, 'A New Beginning', speech delivered at Cairo University, 4 June 2009.

Razack, Sherene, 'A Site/Sight We Cannot Bear: The Racial/Spatial Politics of Banning the Muslim Woman's Niqab', *Canadian Journal of Women and the Law*, vol. 30, no. 1, 2018, pp. 169–89.

Scott, Joan Wallach, 'Big Think Interview with Joan Wallach Scott', *Big Think*, 10 August 2010, https://bigthink.com/videos/big-think-interview-with-joan-wallach-scott

Scott, Joan Wallach, *The Politics of the Veil*, Princeton University Press, Princeton, NJ, 2007.

Shirazi, Faegheh, *Brand Islam: The Making and Commodification of Piety*, University of Texas Press, Austin, TX, 2016.

Zakaria, Rafia, *Veil*, Bloomsbury Academic, London, 2017.

Zuhur, Sherifa, *Revealing Reveiling: Gender Ideology in Contemporary Egypt*, SUNY Press, Albany, NY, 1992.

4 Proxy Wars

Ahmed, Leila, *A Border Passage: From Cairo to America – A Woman's Journey*, Farrar, Straus and Giroux, New York, 1999, p. 11.

Ahmed, Leila, *A Quiet Revolution: The Veil's Resurgence, from the Middle East to America*, Yale University Press, New Haven, 2011.

Aly, Remona, 'UK Mosques Must Make Space for Women – Not Turn Us Away", *Guardian*, 19 February 2018, https://www.theguardian.com/commentisfree/2018/feb/19/british-muslim-women-open-mosque-initiative

Barlas, Asma, *Re-Understanding Islam: A Double Critique*, Spinoza Lectures, Van Gorcum, Amsterdam, 2008.

Baxendale, Rachel, 'Sex Segregation Not Condemned', *The Australian*, 26 April 2013.

REFERENCES

Bhatt, Chetan, 'Human Rights Activism and Salafi-Jihadi Violence', *International Journal of Human Rights*, 2017, https://doi.org/10.1080/1364 2987.2017.1314643

Bolt, Andrew, 'I Would Not Trust Parents With the Power to So Mutilate Their Children', *Herald Sun*, 11 February 2012, www.blogs.news.com.au/heraldsun/andrewbolt/index.php/heraldsun/comments/i_would_not_trust_parents_with_the_power_to_so_mutilate_their_children

Bolt, Andrew, 'Women at the Back: Giving in to Islam at Melbourne Uni', *Herald Sun*, 26 April 2013, www.blogs.news.com.au/heraldsun/andrewbolt/index.php/heraldsun/comments/women_at_the_back_giving_in_to_islam_at_melbourne_uni/

Bone, Pamela, 'Why We Stay Mute on Islamic Sex Apartheid', *The Australian*, 7 December 2007.

Chesler, Phyllis, *The Death of Feminism: What's Next in the Struggle for Women's Freedom?*, Palgrave Macmillan, New York, 2005.

Dux, Monica and Zora Simic, *The Great Feminist Denial*, Melbourne University Press, Carlton, 2008.

Farris, Sara R., *In the Name of Women's Rights: The Rise of Femonationalism*, Duke University Press, Durham, NC, and London, 2017.

Hamzić, Vanja, *Sexual and Gender Diversity in the Muslim World*, I.B. Tauris, London and New York, 2016.

Hirsi Ali, Ayaan, *Nomad: From Islam to America: A Personal Journey Through the Clash of Civilizations*, Free Press, New York, 2010.

Hirsi Ali, Ayaan, 'Why Don't Feminists Fight For Muslim Women?', video lecture, PragerU, 27 June 2016, https://www.prageru.com/sites/default/files/courses/transcripts/ali-why_dont_feminists_fight_for_muslim_women-transcript_0.pdf

James, Clive, 'A Veil of Silence Over Murder', *Standpoint*, September 2009.

Jeffreys, Sheila, *Gender Hurts: A Feminist Analysis of the Politics of Transgenderism*, Routledge, New York, 2014.

Kundnani, Arun, *The Muslims Are Coming! Islamophobia, Extremism and the Domestic War on Terror*, Verso, London, 2014.

Kyriacou, Kate, 'Transsexual Tracie Loses Lesbian Party Bias Case', *Sunday Mail* (SA), 25 April 2009, www.news.com.au/national/transexual-tracie-loses-lesbian-party-bias-case/story-e6frfkp9-1225704089302

Lévy, Bernard-Henri, 'Pakistan and Ayaan Hirsi Ali Are the Front Lines in the War on Terror', *New Perspectives Quarterly*, 15 April 2008.

Manning, Sanchez, 'Our Swimming Pond is NOT gender-fluid: Fury of Hampstead Heath ladies as men identifying as women are allowed into their famous bathing lake', *Daily Mail*, 31 December 2017, https://www.dailymail.co.uk/news/article-5223641/Hampstead-ladies-say-swimming-pond-not-gender-fluid.html

Moghadam, Valentine M., 'Islamic Feminism and Its Discontents: Toward a Resolution of the Debate', *Signs*, vol. 27, no. 4 (summer 2002), pp. 1135–71.

Okin, Susan Moller, 'Is Multiculturalism Bad for Women?' in Joshua Cohen and Matthew Howard (eds), *Is Multiculturalism Bad for Women?*, Princeton University Press, Princeton, NJ, 1999.

REFERENCES

Sisters in Islam, 'The SIS Story', http://sistersinislam.org.my/page.php?35

Steinitz, Jenny, and Olly Hudson, '"I Don't Believe in Transphobia": Germaine Greer Speaks Out at the Union', *Cambridge Student*, 26 January 2015, www.tcs.cam.ac.uk/news/0033654-i-don-t-believe-in-transphobia-germaine-greer-speaks-out-at-the-union.html

Stephen, Sarah, 'A Woman's Place is in the Struggle: Lesfest Restricts Attendance, Sparks Debate', *Green Left Weekly*, 22 October 2003, www.greenleft.org.au/node/28846

Trad, Keysar, 'Why Muslim Women Need their Own Space: An Insider's View', *Crikey*, 24 November 2008, www.crikey.com.au/2008/11/24/why-muslim-women-need-their-own-space-an-insiders-view

Wadud, Amina, *Inside the Gender Jihad: Women's Reforms in Islam*, OneWorld Publications, Oxford, 2006.

5 Invisible Menace

Abu-Lughod, Lila, *Do Muslim Women Need Saving?*, Harvard University Press, Cambridge, MA, 2013.

Alibhai-Brown, Yasmin, *Refusing the Veil*, Biteback Publishing Ltd, London, 2014.

Allen, Liz, 'FactCheck Q&A: The Facts on Birth Rates for Muslim Couples and Non-Muslim Couples in Australia', *The Conversation*, 24 July 2017, https://theconversation.com/factcheck-qanda-the-facts-on-birth-ratesfor-muslim-couples-and-non-muslim-couples-in-australia-81183

Barlas, Asma, *'Believing Women' in Islam: Unreading Patriarchal Interpretations of the Qur'an*, University of Texas Press, Austin, TX, 2002.

Bawer, Bruce, *While Europe Slept: How Radical Islam is Destroying the West from Within*, Doubleday, New York, 2006.

Blee, Kathleen, *Inside Organized Racism: Women in the Hate Movement*, University of California Press, Oakland, 2003.

Bordo, Susan, *Unbearable Weight: Feminism, Western Culture and the Body*, University of California Press, Oakland, 2003.

Courbage, Youssef and Emmanuel Todd, trans. George Holoch, Jr, *A Convergence of Civilizations: The Transformation of Muslim Societies Around the World*, Columbia University Press, New York, 2011.

Demirci, Tuba and S.A. Somel, 'Women's Bodies, Demography, and Public Health: Abortion Policy Perspectives in the Ottoman Empire of the Nineteenth Century', *Journal of the History of Sexuality*, vol. 17, issue 3, University of Texas, 2008, pp. 377–420.

Devine, Miranda, 'Sharia Apologist's Taxpayer Tour a Wasteful Disgrace', *Daily Telegraph*, 18 February 2017, http://www.dailytelegraph.com.au/rendezview/miranda-devine-sharia-apologists-taxpayer-tour-a-wasteful-disgrace/news-story/8f28921546c9af174f6bc5e08e7c7479

Eberstadt, Nicholas, 'The Islamic World's Quiet Revolution', *Foreign Policy*, 9 March 2012, www.foreignpolicy.com/2012/03/09/the-islamic-worlds-quiet-revolution

Elder, John, 'So This Is Easter: Melbourne Faces off at Anti-Islam Rally as Police on Horseback Hold Factions Apart', *Sunday Age*, 5 April 2015.

REFERENCES

Embury-Dennis, T., 'French Town's Decision to Ban Pork-free School Meals Branded "anti-Muslim"', *Independent*, 9 January 2018, https://www.independent.co.uk/news/world/europe/pork-free-school-meals-ban-substitute-france-town-anti-muslim-islamophobic-halal-beaucaire-a8149976.html

Färber, Alexa (ed.), *Islamic Community Life in Berlin*, Berlin Senate for Integration and Migration, Berlin, 2006.

Farrell, Paul, 'Gun Owners Who Made Video of Grand Mufti Effigy Being Shot Face Calls for Ban', *Guardian*, 4 August 2016, https://www.theguardian.com/australia-news/2016/aug/04/gun-owners-who-made-video-of-grand-mufti-effigy-being-shot-face-calls-for-ban

Fekete, Liz, 'Breivik, the Conspiracy Theory and the Oslo Massacre', Briefing Paper No. 5, Institute of Race Relations, London, 1 September 2011.

Hawkins, Oliver (producer), 'Muslim Demographics: The Truth', *More or Less*, BBC Radio 4, 7 August 2009.

Heneghan, Tom, 'Will PEW Muslim Birth Rate Study Finally Silence the "Eurabia" Claim?', Reuters, 27 January 2011, http://blogs.reuters.com/faithworld/2011/01/27/will-pew-muslim-birth-rate-study-finally-silence-the-eurabia-claim/

Hussein, Shakira, 'Halal Chops and Fascist Cupcakes: On Cultural Diversity and the Weaponisation of Food', *Meanjin*, Autumn 2017, https://meanjin.com.au/essays/halal-chops-and-fascist-cupcakes/

Hussein, Shakira, 'Not Eating the Muslim Other: Halal Certification, Scaremongering, and the Racialisation of Muslim Identity', *International Journal for Crime, Justice and Social Democracy*, vol. 4, no. 3, 5 October 2015, https://www.crimejusticejournal.com/article/view/250/196

Ipsos MORI, 'Perceptions Are Not Reality: 10 Things Australia and the World Get Wrong about Society', www.ipsos.com.au/perceptions-are-not-reality-10-things-australia-and-the-world-get-wrong-about-society/

Islam 4 Infidels, 'Muslims Outbreeding Us', 20 April 2014, www.islam4infidels.com/muslims-outbreeding-us/

Jay, Christopher, 'For the Good of the Nation', *Griffith Review*, edn 10, 2004.

Meers, Daniel, 'Martin Place Siege: Hostages Taken in Lindt Chocolate Shop by Armed Robber, *Daily Telegraph*, 14 December 2014, www.dailytelegraph.com.au/news/martin-place-siege-hostages-taken-in-lindt-chocolate-shop-by-armed-robber/story-fni0cx4q-1227156245751

Millar, Erica, '"Too Many": Anxious White Nationalism and the Biopolitics of Abortion', *Australian Feminist Studies*, vol. 30, issue 83, 2015.

Muehlenberg, Bill, 'Creeping Sharia Law in Australia', *News Weekly*, 15 October 2011.

Nachmani, Amikam, *Haunted Presents: Europeans, Muslim Immigrants and the Onus of European-Jewish Histories*, Manchester University Press, Manchester, 2017.

Nussbaum, Martha, *The New Religious Intolerance: Overcoming the Politics of Fear in an Anxious Age*, Harvard University Press, Cambridge, MA, 2012.

Okin, Susan Moller, 'Gender, the Public and the Private', in David Held (ed.), *Political Theory Today*, Stanford University Press, Stanford, 1991.

Pateman, Carole, 'Feminist Critiques of the Public/Private Dichotomy', in Carole Pateman, *The Disorder of Women: Democracy, Feminism and Political Theory*, Stanford University Press, Stanford, 1989.

Pearse, Guy, 'Comment: Dick Smith's Population Crisis', *The Monthly*, June 2011.

Peatling, Stephanie, 'Abortion will Lead to Muslim Nation', *SMH*, 14 February 2006.

Poonam, Snigdha, 'The Cult of the Hindu Cowboy', *Granta* 137, December 2016, https://granta.com/cult-hindu-cowboy/

Simmons, Tracy, 'Jihawg Bullets Designed to Send Muslims "Straight to Hell"', *Huffington Post*, 24 June 2013, https://www.huffingtonpost.com/2013/06/22/pork-laced-bullets-designed-to-send-muslims-straight-to-hell_n_3480150.html

Spencer, Robert, 'Halal Certification Boss Widely Reported as Having Left Sydney Café Just Before Siege Now Denies Having Been There', *Jihad Watch*, 18 December 2014, www.jihadwatch.org/2014/12/halal-certification-boss-widely-reported-as-having-left-sydney-cafe-just-before-jihad-siege-began-now-denies-having-been-there

6 'Jihadi Brides' and Chicks with Sticks

Abdel-Magied, Yassmin, 'I Tried to Fight Racism By Being A Model Minority – And Then It Backfired', *Teen Vogue*, 26 September 2017.

Amnesty International, *Escape from Hell: Torture and Sexual Slavery in Islamic State Captivity in Iraq*, Amnesty International Ltd, London, 2014.

Azzam, Ismail, 'Moroccan Woman Mistaken for Paris Jihadi: I Live in Continuous Fear', CNN, 23 November 2015, https://edition.cnn.com/2015/11/23/africa/paris-female-jihadi-moroccan-woman-photos-sold/index.html

Bishop, Julie, question in Australian Parliament, *Hansard*, 25 February 2015.

Chesler, Phyllis, 'Western Sex Slaves for ISIS: The Twisted Psychology of Jihad Brides', *Breitbart*, 13 August 2014.

'Distraught Man Claims Daughter Being "Held" in Jamia Hafsa', *Dawn*, 23 December 2014, www.dawn.com/news/1152628

El Matrah, Joumanah, personal discussion with the author, 20 April 2015.

Giovanni, Janine di, 'Aafia Siddiqui: The Woman ISIS Wanted to Trade for Foley, then Sotloff', *Newsweek*, 16 September 2014.

Hoyle, Carolyn, Alexandra Bradford and Ross Frenett, *Becoming Mulan?*, Institute for Strategic Dialogue, London, 2015.

Human Rights Watch, 'Iraq: ISIS Escapees Describe Systematic Rape', 14 April 2015.

Hussein, Shakira. 'Dutton's Secret Propaganda Unit', *The Saturday Paper*, 9–15 June 2018, https://www.thesaturdaypaper.com.au/news/politics/2018/06/09/duttons-secret-propaganda-unit/15284664006349

Khan, Sara, 'Families who Fear Isis is Targeting Their Children Urged to Lock Up Their Passports', *Guardian*, 21 February 2015.

Lahoud, Nelly, personal correspondence with the author, 23 September 2014.

REFERENCES

Lahoud, Nelly, 'Can Women Be Soldiers of the Islamic State?', *Survival*, vol. 59, issue 1, 31 January 2017, pp. 61–78.

Penberthy, David, 'Australia is not their home anymore', *Herald Sun*, 30 May 2015.

Qazi, Raheel, personal interview with the author, 2014.

Smith, Peter, 'The Elusive "Moderate Muslim"', *Quadrant Online*, 24 January 2015.

Von Knop, Katharina, *The Female Jihad: Al Qaeda's Women*, Program on Terrorism and Security Studies, George C. Marshall European Center for Security Studies, Gamisch, Germany, 2007.

Winter, Charlie, and Devorah Margolin, 'The Mujahidat Dilemma: Female Combatants and the Islamic State', *CTC Sentinel*, vol. 10, issue 7, August 2017, https://ctc.usma.edu/the-mujahidat-dilemma-female-combatants-and-the-islamic-state/

Conclusion

Ghazelbash, Daniel, 'Why Europe Shouldn't Follow Australia's Lead on Immigration', *The Conversation*, https://theconversation.com/why-europe-shouldnt-follow-australias-lead-on-asylum-seekers-90304

Henderson, Anna, and Chris Uhlmann, 'Syrian Migrant Crisis: Christians to Get Priority as Abbott Faces Pressure to Take in More Refugees', *ABC News*, 8 September 2015, http://www.abc.net.au/news/2015-09-08/christians-to-get-priority-in-syrian-refugee-intake/6757110

Isaacs, Mark, 'There's No Escape from Australia's Refugee Gulag', *FP*, 30 April 2018, https://foreignpolicy.com/2018/04/30/theres-no-escape-from-australias-refugee-gulag/

Moaveni, Azadeh, 'How the Trump Administration Is Exploiting Iran's Burgeoning Feminist Movement', *New Yorker*, 9 July 2018, https://www.newyorker.com/news/news-desk/how-the-trump-administration-is-exploiting-irans-burgeoning-feminist-movement

Polakow-Suransky, Sasha, 'How Europe's Far Right Fell In Love With Australia's Immigration Policy', *Guardian*, 12 October 2017, https://www.theguardian.com/world/2017/oct/12/how-europes-far-right-fell-in-love-with-australias-immigration-policy

Slovic, Paul, Daniel Västfjäll, Arvid Erlandsson and Robin Gregory, 'Iconic Photographs and the Ebb and Flow of Empathetic Responses to Humanitarian Disasters', PNAS, 10 January 2017, http://www.pnas.org/content/early/2017/01/09/1613977114.full

Spindler, William, '2015: The Year of Europe's Refugee Crisis', *UNHCR Tracks*, 8 December 2015, http://tracks.unhcr.org/2015/12/2015-the-year-of-europes-refugee-crisis/

Taylor, Adam, 'New Charlie Hebdo Cartoon Suggests Dead Three-year-old Refugee Aylan Kurdi Would Have Become Sexual Attacker', *Sydney Morning Herald*, 14 January 2016, https://www.smh.com.au/world/new-charlie-hebdo-cartoon-suggests-dead-threeyearold-refugee-aylan-kurdi-would-have-become-sexual-attacker-20160114-gm6893.html

INDEX